The New Gypsy Caravan

Build a Gypsy Caravan

by

Timothy Lemke

www.amvardo.com

"There's real life for you, embodied in that little cart."

Many of us would like to be Toad in the famous book by Kenneth Grahame , Wind in the Willows,. *Toad exclaims to Ratty, "'There's real life for you, embodied in that little cart. The open road, the dusty highway, the heath, the common, the hedgerows, the rolling downs! Camps, villages, towns, cities! Here to-day, up and off to somewhere else to-morrow! Travel, change, interest, excitement! The whole world before you, and a horizon that's always changing! "*

Toad explains the the fantasy of the caravan as well as anyone. Who can resist? Not me!

3D Illustrations by Peter Lemke

Editor Molly Lemke

Photographs by Peter Lemke

ISBN: 978-1-4303-0270-4

Copyright 2006 by Timothy Lemke

Printed in the United States of America

My thanks to my family, Tina, Molly, Ian and Peter, for their patience, help and encouragement to me in building carvans and writing this book.

Table of Contents

Introduction

The New Gypsy Caravan is a low cost, light weight travel trailer. It is easy to assemble on existing trailer frames and is capable of being towed by a small car or truck. It can easily accommodate two adults and a child.

My interest in Gypsy Caravans came out of a real need. I was looking for a better way for our family to go camping. Our antique van was ready to be retired and we had no good way to transport our camping equipment and to accommodate our growing children's needs. In addition, the only reliable transportation was an underpowered mini-SUV, which precluded any conventional RV's. Furthermore, the idea of a conventional RV was not particularly appealing. We are tent campers, who believe that much of the experience of living in the out doors is lost in a "tin can" trailer. In addition, we needed something easy to haul. At first I thought that I would build it myself and began studying various methods of light weight construction. I then considered looking at past methods, and I thought of researching Gypsy caravans. Like many people, the caravan had a romantic attraction for me, promising unlimited adventure and freedom.

Research for this idea uncovered three excellent books as sources on caravans. These are ***The English Gypsy Caravan*** by Ward-Jackson and Harvey, ***Making Model Gypsy Caravans*** by Thompson and ***How to Build a BowTop*** by Walter Lloyd. Although the first two books have provided a wealth of detailed information about the history and construction of caravans, it was Walter Lloyd's small modest book that has yielded the most useful information relating directly to the project.

I decided to adapt this design of a horse-drawn caravan to my needs. Surprisingly, there were relatively few changes that needed to be made. I wanted to use a standard utility trailer as my undercarriage. It turned out that the Lloyd design almost precisely fit a standard 4 'x 8' trailer. I did, however, make several minor changes. The front and rear of the caravan reversed to make it easier to access the caravan while it was still attached to a vehicle, and I added full panels on the ends, to make it more like a standard Bow Top design rather than an Open Lot design. This design seemed to be more practical for automotive transportation. I also used different wood types readily available in the U.S, and used a polyester canvas material for the roof, rather than cotton canvas as Walter Lloyd had used. Other than these changes, the caravan was a close interpretation of the Lloyd design.

The Original Gypsy Caravan with Harry the dog

It took several months of intermittent work to build my new caravan, and by Spring of 2001 it was ready for its maiden voyage, a three hundred mile round trip to fish for Rockfish on the Chesapeake Bay. In spite of skepticism by friends and relatives, the caravan made the trip without incident. In fact, it was easy to haul and was stable on the road, even with crosswinds.

Over the next several years the caravan made numerous trips, over mountains, along the seashore and over the brick paved back streets of the city. The caravan was a welcome refuge from the heat of the day, the cold at night and the rain during storms. Everywhere it went the caravan attracted smiles and attention. People at one campground that we visited looked forward to its return every year.

The caravan was popular everywhere we went. It occurred to me that it might be a good idea to make these caravans readily available to people. Although the Walter Lloyd design was a good one, I felt that it might be able to be improved by using more advanced materials and design to make the caravan even lower in cost and more adaptable to travel over highways. In addition, the caravan should be easy to build and not require any special woodworking skills . The decoration of the caravan is minimized, inviting customized painting and carvings to be added by owner-artists. It also should be able to be easily modified to suit a variety of needs.

With its timeless design, it could be used in reenactments of various periods including medieval, colonial, frontier and civil war. With some modifications, it might also be used as a retail sales tent for arts and crafts fairs or for a small food concession, and is ideal for equestrian events.

The caravan is attractive enough to be parked in the back yard and used as a spare bedroom, playhouse or hide-away for a relaxing nap on a fall afternoon. Many English homes use Gypsy caravans as a focal point for their backyard gardens.

The Gypsies (The Rom)

The following is a brief history of the Gypsies (Rom) and the development of the Gypsy Caravan.

Descended from an ancient warrior class from India, the Gypsies arrived in Europe during the late 15th and early 16th centuries. They migrated through Persia (Iran), Armenia and eventually to Europe. Today, there are over 10 million Gypsies in Europe, mainly in Romania, Hungary, Bulgaria, and Spain. Their dark coppery skin, black hair, and exotic clothing led people to believe that they were from Egypt, and were called “Gyptians” and eventually Gypsies, but they call themselves the "Rom".

Gypsies throughout history have resisted assimilation into the societies in which they lived and have been called "The Least Obedient People in the World". People around the world believed that they stole children, were thieves and practiced witchcraft and magic. As a consequence, Gypsies have been persecuted throughout history and many of them have been exiled or murdered for their lifestyle and beliefs. As many as a million were victims of the Holocaust.

American Gypsies

Gypsies have been in America since around 1640. They were forbidden to immigrate as free people, so they sold themselves as indentured servants to gain entry to America.

Many of these Gypsies came from the Palatinate region of Germany, and with their dark eyes and hair, became known as the "Black Dutch". In the 18th century, many of these Gypsies congregated in the Lancaster, York and Lebanon areas of Pennsylvania and later, some of them moved into the mountainous areas, where they often intermarried with the local population.

Later migration brought Gypsies from southern and eastern Europe and they worked as horse traders, fortune tellers, show people and animal trainers. Often they were able to maintain their extended families, and were led by a hereditary leader. Some of these communities still exist, and its members are often involved in the trade of used cars and trucks. There are over one million Gypsies living in America today.

A Brief History of the Vardo

Until the mid 19th century the Rom lived in tents or "benders" as they moved from place to place. These nomadic structures were similar to modern day dome tents. They used bent saplings as the primary structure. The ends were pushed into the ground and bent over to form a framework. They may have been joined at the top or formed in arches to form either a rectangular or circular floor plan. The framework was then covered with a weatherproof fabric such as canvas.

The Gypsies hauled their belongings in small wagons or "carts" and sometimes slept in or underneath them.

The caravan or vardo,"living wagon" in the Romany language, has evolved over the centuries to its present highly developed form. Covered wagons similar in design to the Vardos, with fabric covered arched roofs, go back to at least Roman times.

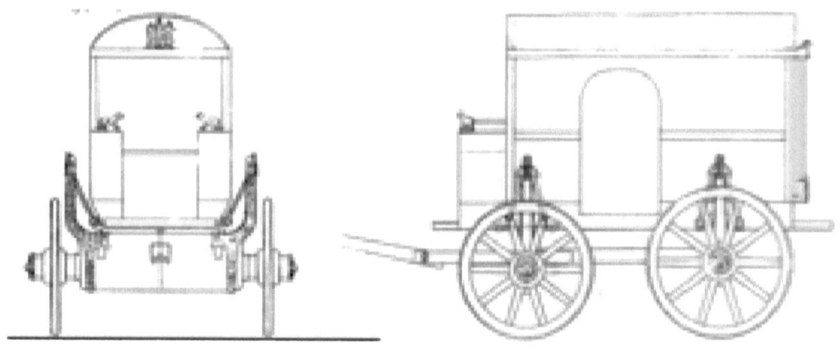

Roman Wagon

Arched wagons are often depicted in Medieval art. However, they were not true living wagons and were used for general transportation.

Medieval Wagon
From *Life In the Middle Ages,*

In America, the "covered wagon" that carried carried settlers Westward, as well as the familiar "chuck wagon" have a similar construction.

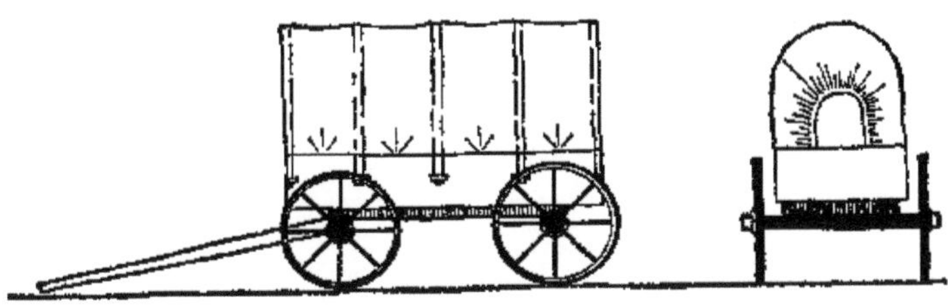

Covered Wagon

By the late 1700's, paved roads were built throughout much of Europe. It is believed that the first living wagons were developed in France for showmen and circus people. These were large wagons that were pulled by teams of horses. By the mid 1800's the living wagons became smaller and the number of horses required to pull them less. The Gypsy caravans have been in existence since around the 1850s and some of the most advanced forms evolved in the British Isles.

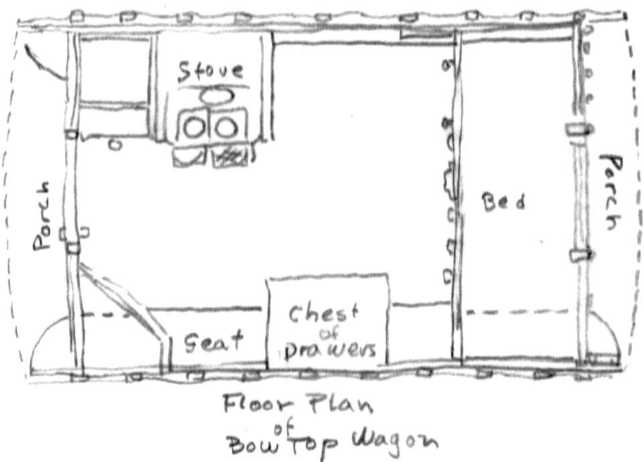

The Gypsy wagons share a number of characteristics, The caravan was specifically designed for comfortable nomadic living. A typical caravan was a four wheeled vehicle that was pulled by a single horse. It tended to have a standard floor plan with a set of drawers to the left and a small stove and mirror to the right, along with a seat and a chest of drawers. Beyond this was a bed, which was sometimes partitioned from the rest of the caravan.

It had an internal stove that was primarily used for heating, and had movable steps for entry.

Many of these Gypsy caravans were home-built, but around 1880, several dedicated makers of gypsy caravans evolved. These wagon makers made some of the most beautiful gypsy caravans ever built.

The Burton Wagon

The Gypsy caravan evolved from the "Burton" wagon, used by showmen and circus people of the mid 19th century. There were not always distinct differences between wagons used by show people and the those preferred by the Gypsies. The Burton wagon, with its small wheels was generally unsuitable for the Gypsies. They needed to be able to travel the rough back roads and fields of the countryside.

Reading Wagon

The use of a single horse mandated that the gypsy caravan be low in weight, but rugged enough to withstand off-road travel, and the Reading wagon came into being. The Reading wagon had a construction similar to the Burton wagon except that it had a narrow body that set between the relatively large wheels. The body was somewhat tapered to increase the room in the wagon. The body was constructed of beaded tongue and groove boards with upright bows and featured an arched roof. The large wheels were required for traveling on rough, unpaved roads, fields and fording streams. Most of them were built by the Dunton family of Reading, England.

The Ledge Wagon

-

The "Ledge" wagons, where the wagon body extended over the large rear wheels, had the advantage of having more elbow room. The ledges were supported by ornate brass brackets. The roofs of these wagons were of solid, slightly arched construction and were extended over each end to form porches. The roofs of the porches were supported by ornate scrollwork cast iron brackets. The roof could be almost 12 feet high. The Ledge wagons were highly decorated, often with gilded carvings.

The Bow Top Wagon

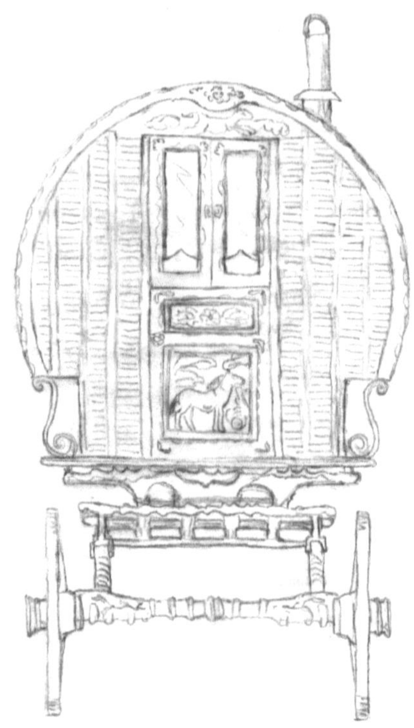

The final development was the "Bow Top", which had the same basic construction as the "Ledge" wagon, but had a light weight canvas top supported by a bowed wooden frame. It seems that it was in this design that the bent saplings of the "bender tent" came together with the "Ledge" wagon. It, like the Ledge, had carved and decorated front and backwalls constructed of thin tongue and groove boards. The roof under the canvas was lined with chenille, "Welsh plaid" or Tartan fabric. Often the top was insulated with carpet or felt. Of all the designs, because of its light weight top, it was the least likely to turn over. The green canvas top was also less noticeable when it was parked in a wooded area.

At the end of the 19th century, an even simpler and lower cost version of the wagon evolved. It was called the Open Lot or Yorkshire Bow. It was built on existing carts featuring an open front with canvas curtains. These were built in some quantity until the 1930's and were almost exclusively used by the Rom.

Decoration and Painting

The nomadic lifestyle of the Gypsies was not amenable to developing the skills required for wagon building, although they sometimes participated in the carving and painting of the wagons. Some of the best decorations were done by the Gypsies.

Much of the value of the caravan was in their elaborate carvings, paintings, and gold leaf. Horses, lions and gryphons along with grapes, sunflowers, and other floral designs were common motifs. The maker of the wagon was identified with specific designs. Many of the wagons had elaborate scrollwork painting that was highlighted by extensive gold leaf on the carvings.

The background colors were typically yellow for the Burton wagons, crimson with gold leaf for the Reading and Ledge wagons and green for the Bow tops, although all combinations of colors can be seen in past examples.

Interiors

The interiors of the wagons most often had varnished natural finish, or were painted with graining to enhance the paint finish. Although some were rough, many of the caravans were well appointed with gold leaf and premium hardwood cabinets filled with silverware and china. The caravan had small iron stoves that were primarily used for heating, but could also be used for cooking in bad weather.

Vardo Life

The caravans have been used by nomadic people of all types, including show people, tinkers and peddlers. Many of the caravans travelled in groups, with a typical group having two caravans and a tent. The Gypsies started out their married lives by buying a vardo from a wagon maker. The caravan was considered to be the Gypsy wife's most prized possession. The men usually slept in the tents or under the vardo. The inside was the domain of the women .

When the Gypsies found a place to camp the wise woman of the group would walk around the site with a ceremonial broom and sweep away the unclean spirits.

The vardos were intricately involved in funeral rituals and were often burned after their owner had died.

Most of the cooking was done outside using a tripod and "Dutch Oven".

Dogs, cats, bantam chickens and even caged birds accompanied the nomadic travelers on their journeys.

The Gypsy Vanner

The horses used to pull the caravans were bred specifically by the Rom for the task. They are known as the Gypsy "Vanner"horse or Gypsy Cob horse They were developed by crossbreeding the Friesian, the Clydesdale, the Shire, the Fells Pony and the Dales Pony. They are a compact and colorful draft horse with a long, thick tail and mane, so that it looks like it emerged from a fantasy.

Black and white and brown and white are the most common colors. The horse has a gentle and trustworthy temperment and is particularly gentle with children, at least Gypsy children.

Appleby Fair

One of the places in England where large groups of Romany people still gather is the Appleby Fair. The fair is a week-long horse sale that is held each June in the town of Appleby-in-Westmoreland, Cumbria, along the River Eden. Gypsy families meet up with old friends there to show off their horses and vardos.

The New Gypsy Caravan

The New Gypsy Caravan is a low cost travel trailer capable of being towed by a small vehicle. It is intended to be used as a camper for couples or small families and can be used with tents for larger ones. The caravan can be used to store and transport supplies and equipment.

Whereas the original caravans were designed for single horse power transportation, both on and off the newly paved roads of the mid 19th century, the modern version is intended for high speed automotive travel, while maintaining many of the classic design features of the original.

Design

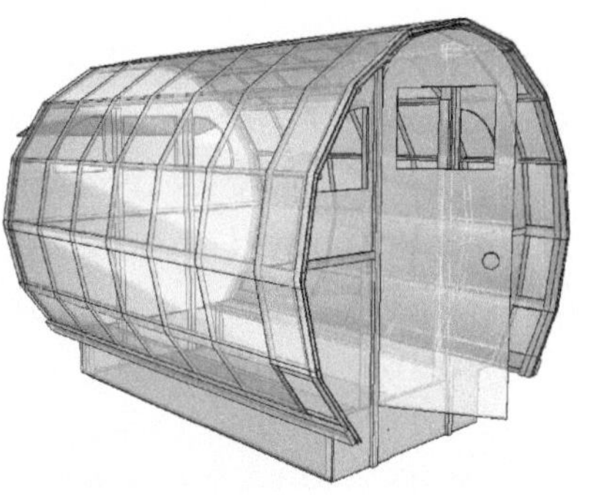

The basic structure and design of the Bow-top caravan has been maintained in the new design. The egg-shaped cross-section of the structure has unique advantages. It is narrow at the base, about four feet, where it fits into a standard sized wagon or utility trailer. The overhang of the ledges widen it almost a foot to five feet, and they provide additional strength and stiffness to the frame. In addition, the ledges provide seating inside of the caravan as well as support for a bed frame. The bow shaped structure of the roof adds an additional foot to the width of the caravan body to around six feet. This additional width literally is "elbow room", since it adds space where it is needed. The caravan becomes wide enough at this point to allow for a bed across the width of the structure. The combination of the bows and runners distributes stresses across the roof structure, resulting in a stiff, structure that is lightweight and forgiving.

Most of the differences between the traditional design and the New Gypsy Caravan are the materials and the building techniques used. This has been done to help reduce the weight and the cost. One important change is that the front and rear of the caravan have been reversed to accommodate the use of a standard trailer rather than a horse. The door is now in the rear of the caravan rather than the front as with the horse drawn version. This was done to make entry and exit easier.

The windows and doors are somewhat different than the original design. In the original "Open Lot" caravans, canvas curtains were used instead of a door. In other designs, fancy "bow windows" were added to the rear, and ornately carved doors were used in the front. A simpler approach is used in the new version, with a light weight door and quarter circle windows on either side. The rear has a similar arrangement, only with a rectangular window instead of a door. A single rear "shutter" is attached to this window combination. The primary function of the shutter is to close off the windows during travel at highway speed to minimize air turbulence and to prevent rain from entering the caravan. It can later be used to shade the windows and to protect against the wind and rain. The complex shapes of plywood end panels and doors are computer designed and fabricated using a computer controlled manufacturing system. The resulting panels are precisely cut and contribute to the low weight and high strength of the structure. The traditional canvas top has been replaced with a dimensionally stable fiberglass reinforced polyethylene fabric that is rot resistant, light weight and low cost.

Adhesives are used throughout the frame construction to prevent potential loosening of the joints caused by the vibrations induced by high speed automotive travel.

The design has been adapted to low cost utility trailers rather than the heavy wooden wheeled under carriages of the past. The low weight and design of the caravan allows it to be used with inexpensive trailers. The rounded shape of the bow top has good aerodynamic characteristics. The shape minimizes instability cause by side winds. The caravan has good towing characteristics since it has an even weight distribution with a low center of gravity.

Although these changes are important, the basic classic design of the vardo, with its unique esthetics and functionality has been maintained.

Build it Yourself

Fully assembled versions will be offered, but they will be available only in limited areas.

The New Gypsy Caravan may be built by either using the plans and instructions provided in this book to build one from scratch, or by purchasing a kit . Drawings and full scale paper templates for the end panels, door and shutter may be purchased from **American Vardo** to aid in the construction of a caravan "from scratch.

Caravan Kits

The kits may be the easiest and most economical way of obtaining a caravan. Typically, the basic kit can be assembled in 20 to 40 hours, although more additional time may be required for finishing, decoration and accessories.

Basic Package - This package contains the essential parts which are either difficult to fabricate or to obtain and include the CNC cut end panels, door, shutters and bows. The bows are made of straight grain poplar and are pre-drilled with the appropriately spaced pilot holes. The detailed plans and this book are included in the kit.

Builder Supplied Materials

In order to keep the costs as low as possible by reducing shipping costs the kit builder will be required to supply the following commonly available materials:

Caulk - High quality -paintable - 2 tubes

Construction Adhesive - 2 tubes

Base Ends and Sides 1" x12" x 8ft. (3)

Floor (4' x 8' , 3/4" plywood)

2x3's for king posts.

1x2's 1x3's 1x4's for runners, and weather boards.

4' x 8' Utility Trailer

Trailer Mounting Hardware (1/4" bolts,nuts and lock washers)

Tools Required

Only simple tools are required for assembly of the enhanced kit. These include:

Power Screw Driver or Electric Drill with driver bit

1/4″ and 1/8″ drill bit for metal and wood

Square | Stapler
Caulking Gun | Utility Knife

Tape Measure

Simple woodworking tools are required to make the slots at the ends of the runners, drill pilot holes and cut the individual pieces to the proper length. Some of the tools that may be required include:

Table Saw or hand saw

Drill

Tape Measure and square

Before You Start

It would be a good idea to read this section completely before you start the construction of the caravan. One of the most important items is the trailer. Ideally, the caravan should be constructed on the trailer, since it is difficult to get the caravan on the trailer after it is built.

The Trailer

Make sure that you read and follow the instructions that came with your trailer.

The first thing to consider is how the trailer will be hauled, and whether a trailer hitch can be installed.

Careful selection of a trailer is important for easy installation of a caravan. Although modifications can be made, it is always desirable to make as few changes as possible.

There are two basic requirements:

The trailer bed should be able to accept a 48"' x 96"' (4 x 8) sheet of plywood. There is a +/- 3/4 inch 1/1/2" tolerance on this requirement. The floor can be trimmed if the trailer is slightly too small, and mounting spacers can be added if it is too large.

If there are side rails on the trailer, they can be no higher than 12" from the surface of the bed. The ledges (seats) of the trailer need to clear the sides. If the sides are somewhat higher than this, the caravan body can be raised by putting 2 x 4' underneath the caravan floor.

Ideally there should be some sort of side rails to attach the trailer to. Many utility trailers have railings supported by vertical uprights. These are good places to secure the caravan body.

The trailer should be relatively level when attached to the vehicle. This means the rear of the trailer or the tongue should not be excessively low.

Make sure the tongue is long enough to allow for a reasonable turning radius and clearance to the vehicle when turning, or when opening the door of the caravan.

Tail and running lights and reflectors should be installed around the trailer.

The low weight and design of the caravan allows it to be used with relatively inexpensive trailers.

If the caravan is to be constructed from a kit, make sure all of the components are received.

Parts

If the caravan is to be made from a kit, there are additional parts that should be made prior to the assembly. These are made from standard lumber that can be obtained from any lumber yard or home center. The precise dimensions for these parts are available from the **drawings** in the back of the book, or from the **plans** included in the kit.

Connectors

Four 2″x2″ pieces are required to connect the elements of the base together. These can be cut from a four foot section of 2″x2″ lumber. A 2″ x 3″ piece could be used as well. These are cut to about 11 1/4″ length.

Glue blocks

The ***glue block***s are used to attach the runners to the end panels. These can be made from the scraps left over from cutting the runners. These should be cut approximately to length. It is important to drill pilot holes in these pieces, since otherwise they will split when they are screwed to the end panels. The ***glue blocks*** can be assembled to the end panels prior to assembly, as shown in the drawings, or after the ***runners*** are assembled. Make sure these are glued to the panels.

Base

The ***base*** is constructed from stand 1″x12″ boards. Five 8′ long boards will be required. Make sure they are 8′ long, and if not trim four of them to the exact length.

The ***base end***s need to be cut from one 8 ft. piece to 45″ length for each.

Three pilot holes are to be drilled at the end of the Base sides and ends.

Pilot holes are also to be drilled along the centerline of the ledges, to aid in locating the ledge to the sides and to prevent splitting.

King Posts

The ***king posts*** are made from four 6ft. Long 2″ x3″ lumber . The King Posts has a 11 1/2″ section3/4″ thick removed at the one end, so that it can fit over the ***base end*** . This is cut from the 3″ width of the lumber.

Runners, Edge Support

The *roof runners,* and the *ledge runners* are made from 10 ft. long 1x4s 1 x 3s and 1 x2s. These are all cut to length -9'3". The *runners* are required to have notches cut into the ends so that they interlock with the corresponding notches on the end panels . The 1" x3" b*ase runners* and the 1"x4" r*idge runner* have notches cut on both sides. The 1"x2" Roof Runners have a single notch on both ends. There are several ways to do this, depending on the types of tools available. The simplest way is to use a 3/8" diameter router to cut the notches. They also may be cut using a saw to cut to the appropriate depth and then a chisel to remove the scrap.

Markings are required on the runners to assist in locating the ***bows***. This can be done by lining up the runners of each size and drawing the lines, using a square, across the batch. The 1"x3" and 1"x4" pieces are marked on their faces, and the 1"x2" pieces are marked on their edges.

Ledge Runner

This somewhat more difficult, since the edge of the board must be cut at an angle. This can be readily done on a table saw. It can also be done using a circular saw, but with a little more difficulty. If a little more than just the edge is removed, there should be no problem. Place a mark 11 5/8" from the one end of the ledge runner. The mark helps to determine the placement of the ledge runner on the ledge board.

Weatherboards

After cutting to length, these only require pilot holes as shown in the drawing. Although not absolutely necessary, they do prevent splitting of the boards during assembly, particularly at the ends.

Trim

The trim components are cut from 8ft. long 1″x2″ pieces. Again, pilot holes should be drilled to prevent splitting - particularly at the ends.

Screws

The screws used are are coated or galvanized decking screws. The screws come in 1 1/4″ and 1 5/8″ lengths. Standard galvanized wood screws are used where 1″ screws are required such as for the bows and for attaching the panels to the base.. 6 x 1″pan head screws with washers are recommended for attaching the bows to the roof runner.

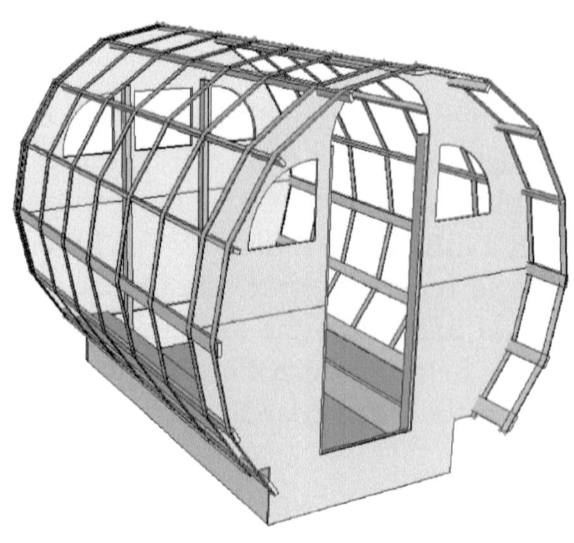

The Assembly Manual

This manual is intended to be a guide for the assembly of caravans built from "scratch" or from kits. Each section is made up of parts, the list of materials and tools required, and assembly drawings. These parts are followed by a description of the assembly procedure, which usually includes a photograph of the assembled component. There are dimensioned drawings at the end of the section. The drawings can be used to fabricate the individual components or simply as guides to help identify the components of a kit.

The caravan be painted at almost any time during its construction.. However, it might be a good idea to prepaint some o f the components such as the base and end panels before starting assembly.

Larger detailed drawings and full scale templates for the end panels are available from **American Vardo** at www.amvardo.com/caravan.

Base End

Description	Size	Qty	Drawing
Base, Ends	1 x 12 x 461/2	2	01
Base Connectors	2 x 2 x 12 in	4	02

Material: Construction Adhesive

Hardware: (12) 1 5/8" Deck Screws

Tools: Screw Driver, Caulking Gun (adhesive)

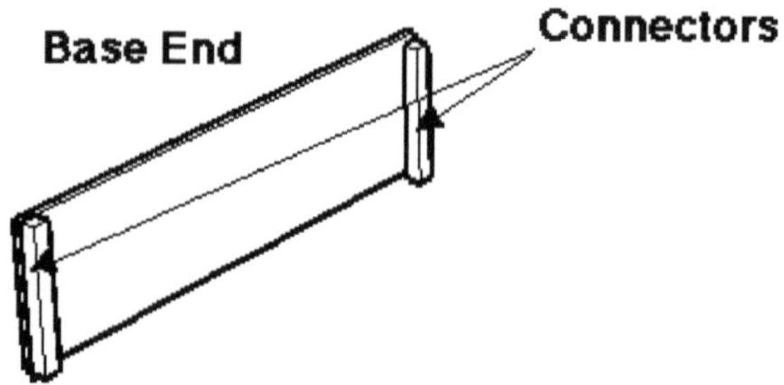

Base End Assembly

The first step of the base assembly is to attach the ***Base Connectors*** to the ***Base Ends***. The Base Connectors are placed on a flat surface, approximately 46 inches apart. A bead of adhesive is applied to the ***Base Connector.*** The Base End is then carefully placed on top of the connectors, making sure that the ends and edges are aligned. There are three pilot holes at the ends of the ***Base End*** boards. Three 1 5/8" deck screws are used to attach each end of the connector to the ***Base End***.

Base Side

Description	Size	Qty	Drawing
______Base, Sides	1 x 12 x 8ft	2	01

Material: Construction Adhesive

Hardware: (12) 1 5/8" Deck Screws,

Tools: Screw Driver, Caulking Gun (adhesive)

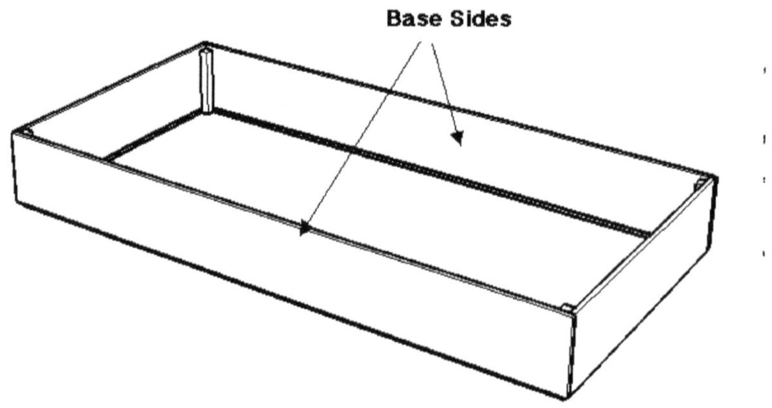

Base Side Assembly

The ***Base Ends*** are attached to the ***Base Sides*** in much the same way. The ***Base Sides*** and the ***Base Ends*** are arranged so that the edges of the ***Base Sides*** are aligned with the edges of the ***Base Ends***. Adhesive is applied to the connector, and the three 1 5/8" deck screws are used to attach the end to the base, making a rectangular box structure.

Floor

Description	Size	Qty	Drawing
Floor	4 x 8 x 3/4	1	03

Material: Construction Adhesive

Hardware: (22) 1 ¼" Deck Screws,

Tools: Screw Driver, Caulking Gun (adhesive)

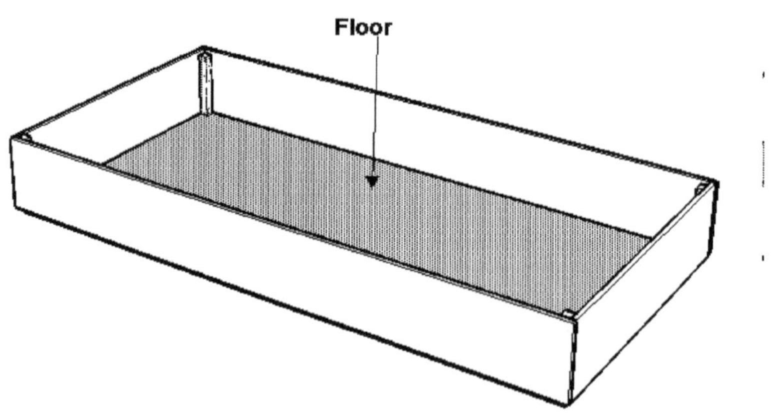

Floor attachment

Place the plywood ***Floor*** on top of the base. Using a chalk line or long straight edge, draw lines along the length the plywood ***Floor*** 3/8 inch from the edges of the long length of the plywood. This is the centerline of where the screws are to be attached. Start at one end of each line and make marks at 2" and at 16 inch increments along the length. These marks indicate where the attachment screws are to be located. Drill 1/8" diameter pilot holes at the marks. Carefully place a bead of adhesive around the edge of the ***Base Assembly***.

Attach the ***Floor*** to the base using 1 1/4 inch deck screws.

Ledge Assembly

Description	Size	Qty	Drawing
Ledges	1 x 12 x 8ft	2	04
Ledge Runner	1 x 3 x 9'3"ft	2	05

Material: Construction Adhesive

Hardware: (12) 1 5/8" Deck Screws,

(12) 1 1/4" Deck Screws

Tools: Screw Driver, Caulking Gun (adhesive)

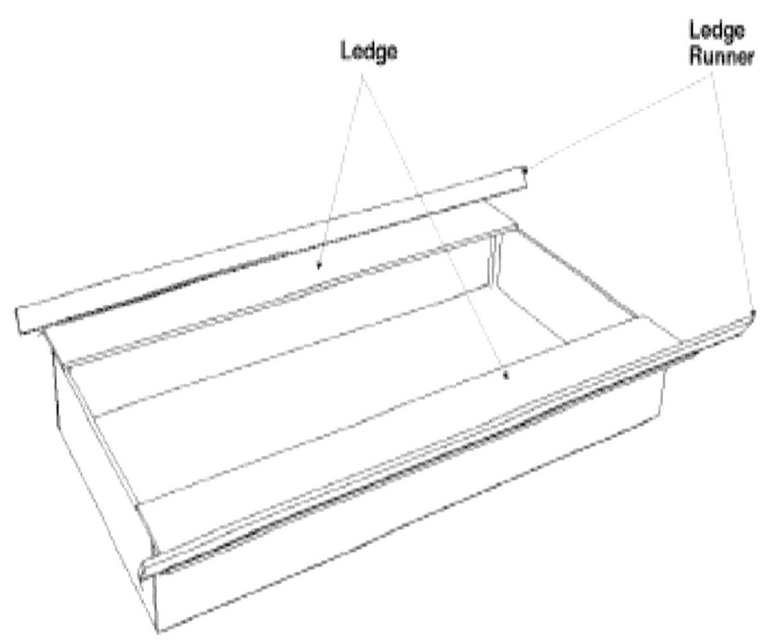

Ledge Assembly

The ***Ledges*** have a series of pilot holes along the midline and a similar series along the one edge. A bead of adhesive is place along the edge. of the ***Ledge*** board, covering the pilot holes . ***The Ledge Runner*** is attached to the ledge by careful positioning it along the pilot holes along the edge of the ***Ledge*** board. The ***Ledge Runner*** will project from the front edge by 3 7/8" and the rear by 11 5/8". Use 1 1/4" screws to attach the runner to the ***Ledge***.

Apply a bead of adhesive along the long edge of the ***Base Assembly***.The ***Ledge assembly*** must be carefully aligned with the top edges of the ***Base Sides.*** These holes are to be carefully aligned with the sides of the base assembly. The holes on the edge should be on the outside of the base frame. Use -1 1/4 inch screws to attach the ***Ledges*** to the ***Sides*** and to the ***End boards***. Attach one end first, and then make sure the other end is properly aligned and use a screw to attach this end. Inspect the holes along the length of the ***Ledge*** to make sure they are over the edge of the **Base Sides**. Again, attach the ***Ledge***

through one of the holes approximately in the middle of the seat. It may be necessary to push on the sides, in case they are slightly warped. With the middle and ends secured, the rest of the screws may be applied.

Assembly of Base to Trailer

If possible, this is the best time to install the base of the caravan to the trailer. The base is easier to move and is more accessible for installing the mounting hardware. After the caravan is completed, it is possible to move it onto a trailer and secure it, but it is much more difficult to do at this stage of construction

This is a critical step in the construction of the Caravan, but since the builder has the choice of trailer, it is difficult to precisely describe how the mount the caravan to the trailer. However, the following are some guidelines on how to do it.

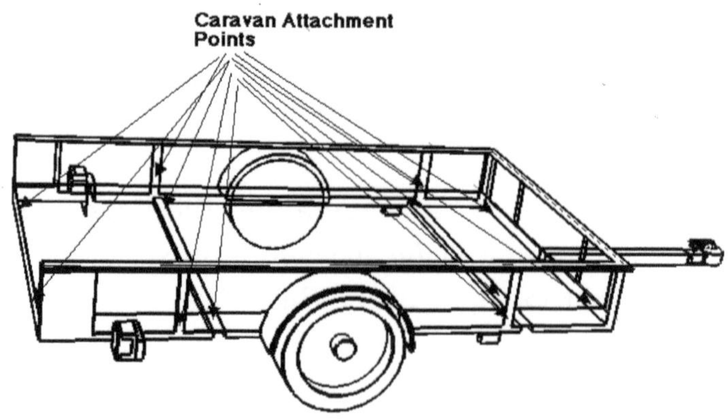

Many trailers of this size have vertical side rails. If this is the case, the caravan can be securely attached to the trailer by the use of "U" bolts. I used 1/4" x 5" "U" bolts in the first caravan that I built. Holes are drilled on

either side of the vertical upright on the trailer and the legs of the "U" bolt are placed over the vertical upright and inserted through the holes in the caravan. The "U" bolt is then secured with washers, lock washers and nuts on the inside of the caravan.

A more direct way of attaching the Caravan is to bolt the floor of the caravan directly to the trailer frame. Typically there are several cross members on the trailer frame to which the caravan may be secured. I have used 1/4" or 5/8" x 1 inch bolts to do this. The best place to locate the bolts is under ledges, so they do not interfere with traffic in the caravan. Two or three bolts may also be located on the ends of the caravan/trailer. Again, the bolts are secured with washers, lock washers and nuts. This should make a very secure installation.

Lower End Panels

Description	Size	Drawing
Lower Rear Panel	6 x 3 x 3/8	07
Lower Front Panel	6 x 3 x 3/8	08

Glue Blocks

Material: Construction Adhesive

Hardware: (24) 1 " wood screws

(8) 1 5/8" deck screws

Tools: Screw driver

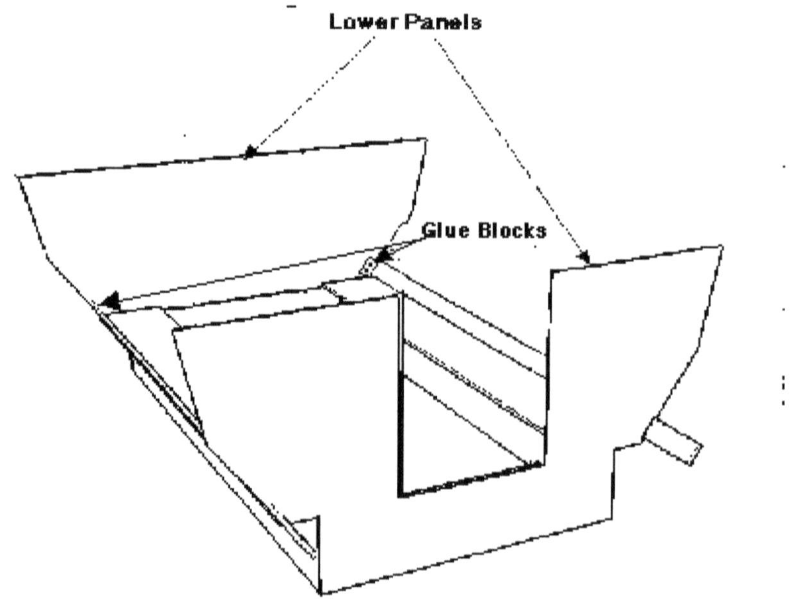

Lower Panel Assembly

Apply adhesive to the ***Base End*** , where the ***Lower Panels*** are to be attached. The ***Front*** and ***Back*** plywood ***End Panels*** are assembled by applying adhesive to the base ends. The ***Lower Front Panel*** and ***Rear Panel*** are aligned with the end of the base assembly. If there are pre-drilled holes in the Base The bottom of the ledge is aligned with the corresponding section of the end panel. These ***End Panels*** are secured to the base using (8) 1 5/8 inch screws and (4) 1 inch wood screws along the mid-line.

Glue Blocks

Glue Blocks are attached to the end panels with 1″ screws, so that the long edge is aligned with the notch at the lower edge of the end panel. This will provide a surface for the ledge runner to be attached. The ***Ledge Runner*** is then screwed to the end blocks using two 1 5/8″deck screws.

King Post

Description	Size	Qty	Drawing
King Posts	2 x 3 x 6 ft	4	06

Material: Construction Adhesive

Hardware: (4) 1 5/8″ deck screws

Tools: Screw driver

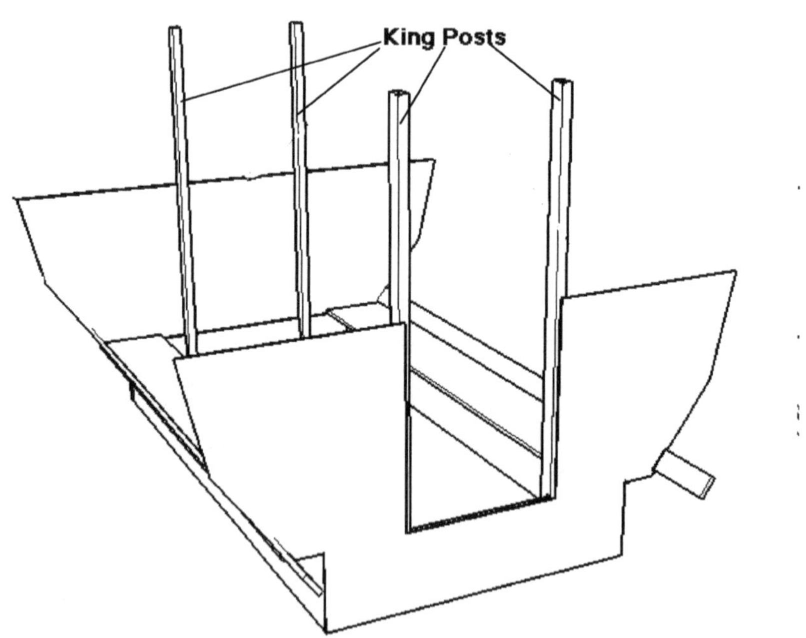

King Post Assembly

The King posts are located so that they are spaced 22" apart or on 23 1/2" centers. These can be aligned with the door opening on the front end panel, but location liens will have to be drawn on the rear end panel perpendicular to the floor, 22"apart.

An adhesive bead is applied to the lower half of the ***King Post***. The king posts are then attached to the panel with 1 5/8 screws inserted through the pilot holes in the panel.

The ***King Post*** should be checked for alignment and be square with the base.

Upper End Panels

Description	Size	Drawing
Upper Front Panel	6 x 3 x 3/8	09
Upper Rear Panel	6 x 3 x 3/8	010

Material: Construction Adhesive

Hardware: (10) 1 5/8" deck screws

Tools: Screw driver, wrench

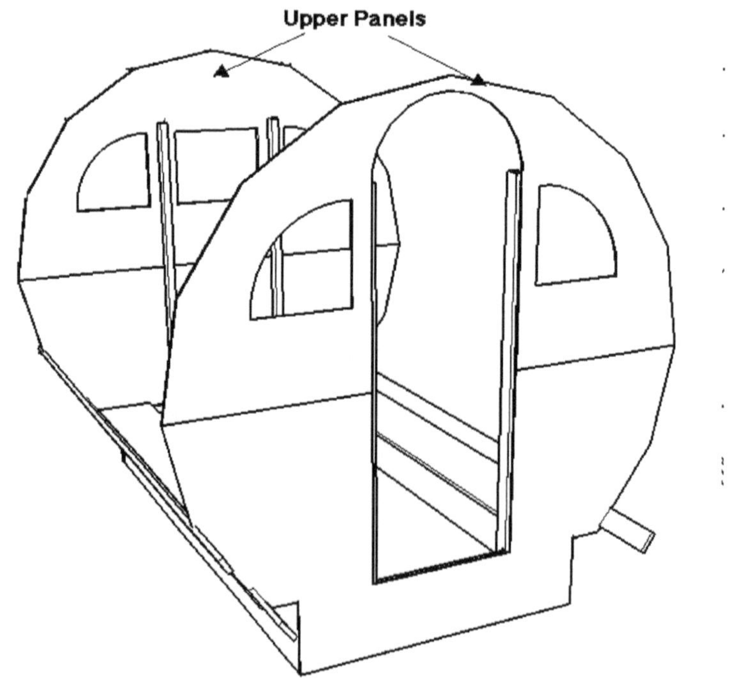

Upper Panel Assembly

An additional adhesive bead is then applied to the top portion of the ***King Post***. If possible, the ***Upper Panel*** can then be aligned with the top edge of the ***Lower Panels***, and the 1/4" holes in the upper section of the plywood piece, if they are present. The ***Upper*** plywood ***Panels*** can be attached to the ***King Post***, using 1 5/8"deck screws. This procedure is done for both ends.

Runners

Parts

Description	Size	Qty	Drawing
Runners,Lower	1 x 3 x 10 ft	4	11
Runners,Upper	1 x 2 x 10 ft	6	12
Runner, Ridge	1 x 4 x 10 ft	1	11
Glue blocks	1 x 2 x 4"	5	02

Material: Construction Adhesive

Hardware: (18) 1 ¼" deck screws

(10) 1″ wood screws

Tools: Screw Driver

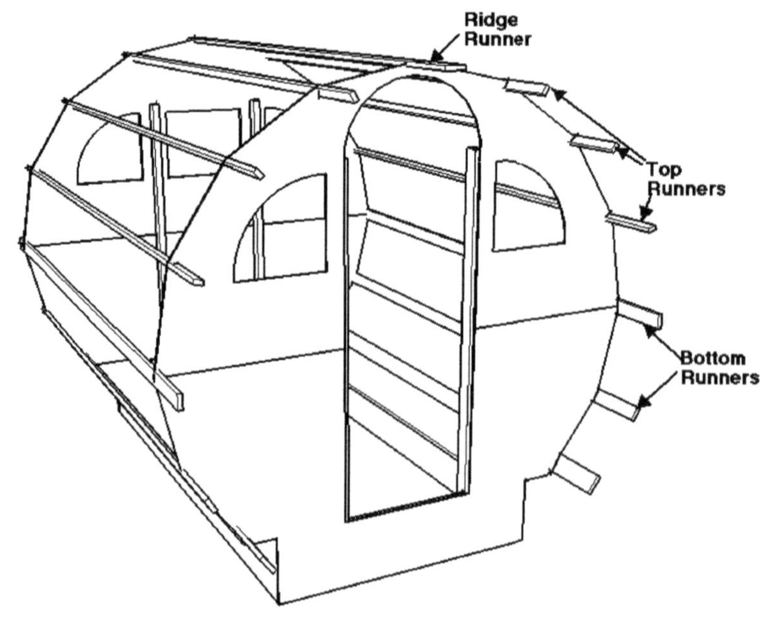

Runner Assembly

Glue Blocks

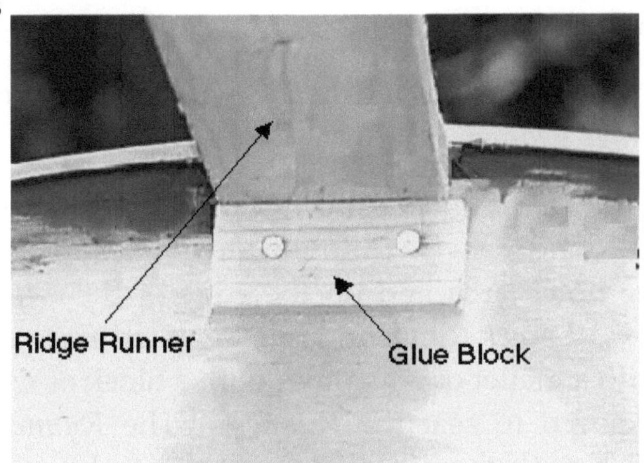

Small blocks of wood, ***Glue Blocks,*** are attached to the ***End Panels*** adjacent to the notches of the lower panel and adjacent to the notch at the very top of the Upper Panel. These ***Glue Block***s are used to secure the runners to the end panel. A small bead of adhesive is applied to the block, and the long edges of the ***Glue Block*** are aligned with the bottom edge of the notch. The block is attached to the panel with two 1"wood screws.

Runner Assembly

Before the ***Runners*** are assembled they need to be marked to indicate the final location of the bows. The ***Lower Runners*** and ***Ridge Runner*** should be marked with a pencil on the flat side of the ***Runners,*** at 16" increments as shown in the drawing.

The 1 x 2 ***Upper Runners*** are similarly marked, but on the edge opposite from the notch.

Make sure the marks can be seen from the outside of the Caravan assembly.

A line should be drawn down the center of the ***Ridge Runner.***

The runners are installed between the front and back end panels. Apply a small amount of adhesive to the notch area and on the edge of the ***Glue Block***. The 1 x 3 ***Lower Runners*** are assembled first. Several taps with a mallet or a hammer with a block of wood might be required to seat the ***Runners***. The ***Runners*** should be flush with the outer edges of the end panels. Two 1 ¼" deck screws are used at each end, to attach the runner to the ***Glue Block***.

The 1 x 2 ***Upper Runners*** are used for the upper section. These are attached simply by applying adhesive to the notch area.

The 1x 4 ***Ridge Runner*** is attached with adhesive and two screws at each end, in the same way as the ***Lower Runners***.

Bows

Parts

Description	Size	Qty	Drawing
Outer Bows	2 x 1/4 x 8 ft	20	14
Inner Bows	2 x 1/4 x 8 ft	4	15

Materials: Construction Adhesive

Caulk

Hardware: Screws (80) #6 1" wood screws

(36) #6 1″ pan head screws with washers

Tools: Screw Driver, Caulking gun

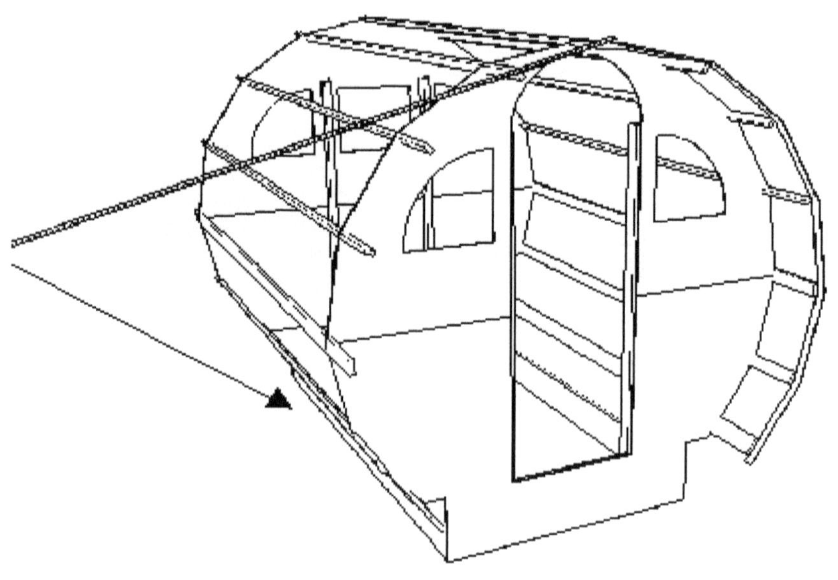

Bow Assembly The assembly of the ***Bows*** is the final step of the frame assembly. This should be done with care, since it will determine the final shape of the bow top. The ***Bow*** assembly should start at both ends with bows first being attached over the junction of the bows and ***End Panels*** and then to the ends of the ***Runners.*** The rest of the ***Bow*** assembly should start from the center and work outward toward both ends. The ***Bows*** are aligned with the marks on the runners to provide the correct spacing. Construction adhesive is applied at each junction between the ***Bows*** and Runners. The pilot hole is aligned with the center of the runner. The ***Bow*** is first attached to the first 1″x 2″ ***Runner*** and then attached to the ***Lower Runners*** and finally the ***Ledge Runners***. The end of the ***Bow*** with two pilot holes is assembled to the ***Ridge Runner.*** Pan head 1″ screws , with washers are recommended for this step, to prevent splitting of the ***Bow*** as it is drawn onto the ***Ridge Runner***. The ***Bow*** is then attached to the remaining two 1″ x 2″ ***Roof Runners*** with 1″ wood screws and construction adhesive.

Additional sets of ***Bows*** are attached to the ends of the ***Runners*** on the inside surface of the ***Runners*** on both ends. These are used to support the cover fabric as it is wrapped around the ends of the roof structure.

Caulk End Panels.

The gap between ***End Panels*** and their associated Bows may require caulking.

Beds and cabinets(Optional)

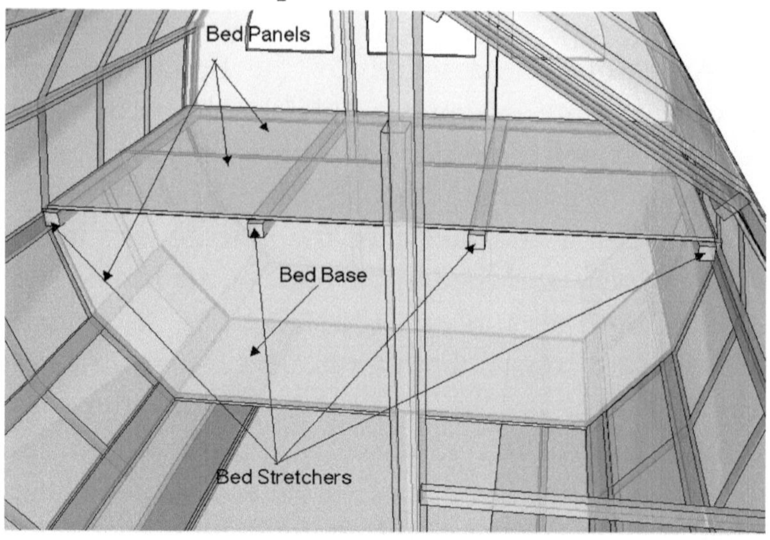

The installation of a bed and cabinets is optional, and may be conveniently done after the basic caravan is completed. However, at this stage, before the outer cover is installed might be the best time to build the bed .
An integral part of a traditional caravan is the bed. The bed takes up almost half of the available space. The unique design of the caravan allows for about six feet of length for the bed extending across the width of the Caravan, even though the trailer is only 4 ft wide . The main axis of the bed is positioned at the widest part of the caravan, about at mid-height. The design of the American Gypsy Caravan's bed uses plywood panels, similar to those on the ends, for the frame. One panel is attached to the ***King Posts*** at the back end of the caravan and the other is positioned at about midway along the length of the caravan, with another midway between the two. A 5' x 4' piece of plywood is attached to the ledges . This is

the floor for the storage area under the bed. The bottom edge of the bed frame panels rest on the plywood base.

The middle panel and the panel on the inner end panel are attached to the bottom runners and are supported by means of "glue blocks" much in the same way as they are attached to the the end panels.

2″ x 2″ stretchers that are notched on the end fit into matching notches on the top edge of the bed end panels. The bed surface can be made up of a single 4′ x 6′ panel or of three 4′ x 2′ panels. The two outer panels may be attached to the stretchers (supports) with 1 1/4" screws The middle one can be left unattached to allow access to the storage area underneath. Openings can be cut in the bed panels to lighten them and to allow access. Cabinet doors could be attached with hinges to make a storage cabinet.

Painting

This would be a good time to paint the frame of the caravan. The edges of the Ledge seats can be rounded and sanded. The traditional caravans were often painted on the outside and sometimes varnished on the inside. The Bows could be varnished, painted or left unfinished.

Roof

Description	Size	Quantity
Inner Liner(optional)		
Insulation(optional)		
Roof Covering	12ft x 16ft	1

Hardware: 1/4" Staples

Tools: Staple Gun

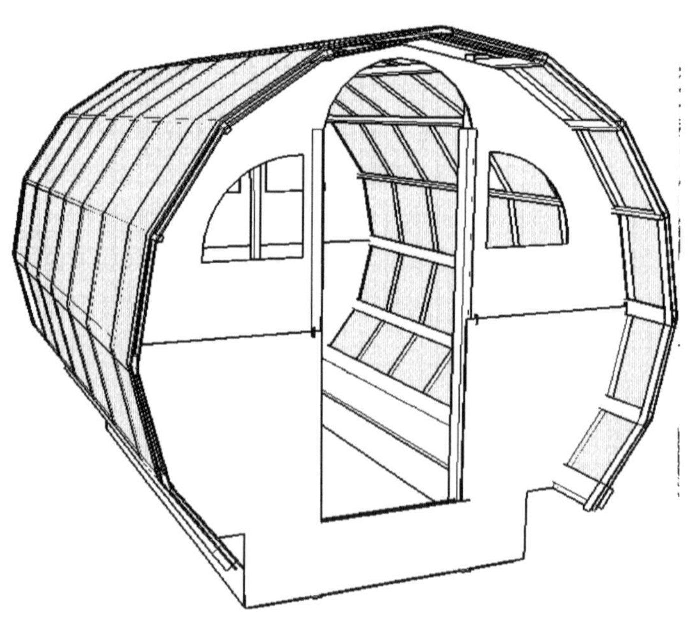

Roof

Inner Liner

An inner liner of an inexpensive fabric can be stapled to the ***Bows*** of the caravan. Traditional caravans used Welch or Tartan plaid material or chenille as a liner.

Insulation

The original Bow Top caravans were insulated from the cold winds and the sun by a felt layer that was installed between the outer canvas cover and an inner Welsh or Scottish plaid liner. If it is expected that the caravan will be used for cold weather camping or in unshaded areas, it might be useful to insulate it as well. Rather than using felt, which is heavy and can absorb moisture, modern insulating materials can be used. One material which has been used successfully is Reflectix™. It is comprised of two layers of plastic "bubble wrap" (visually identical to that used for packaging) laminated between two sheets of plastic protected aluminized foil. It is one of the original and most commonly available radiant heat insulations and can be found at many local hardware and building supply stores.

The insulation would be stapled over the fabric and to the ***Bows***. The ***Roof Cover*** installation would then follow. This three layer roofing would present an attractive interior as well as a weather resistant skin that would buffer the interior of the caravan from temperature extremes of heat or cold.

The roof covering supplied with the standard caravan kits is a 10 ft. x 16 ft fiber reinforced 10 mil thick polyethylene material of a type often used for tarps. This material is strong, lightweight and very low cost and UV resistant.

Drape the ***Roof Cover*** over the Caravan frame so that it is evenly distributed on all sides and the wrinkles are smoothed as much as possible.

Starting at the middle of one side, staple the cover to the ***Edge Support*** . The cover is to be stapled in between the bows and on the ***Bows***, with at least two staples per Bow.

Repeat the stapling process on the other side while applying some tension to the cover to minimize the wrinkles.

The cover is then stapled to both ends by wrapping the material over the edge and the inside bow and stapling it to the *Inside Bow*. Again, after the one end is stapled, apply some tension to minimize wrinkles, as the other end is being stapled.

Alternative Roof Coverings

There are a number of alternatives for the roof covering material used in the kits. Each of them have their own advantages and disadvantages. The reinforced polyethylene material is low cost and low weight, but depending on the climate and exposure to sunlight, this covering may be expected to last only 1-5 years.

The original caravans used cotton canvas as a roofing material. This might be considered for a more authentic appearance. Cotton canvas was used in the past because of its durability and all-weather protection. The canvas had an oily or waxy coating so it didn't absorb water. The coating didn't seal the fabric, so the fabric could breathe. Since canvas wasn't waterproof, it relied on rain water's surface tension between the cotton fibers to keep it from leaking.

Canvas does have the disadvantage of weight, moisture absorption and mildewing.

Polyester canvas has the advantages of lower weight, rot resistance, and recently UV resistant versions have been introduced. These materials can closely approximate the appearance of cotton canvas without some of the disadvantages. My original caravan used a polyester canvas material and it has performed well for over five years. It can be supplied by makers of awnings and marine boat cover, where it is extensively used.

Inner Bows

Description	Size	Qty	Drawing
Inner Bows	1 x 1/4″ x 8′	4	15

Hardware: #6 1 " Wood Screws

Tools: Drill, Screw Driver

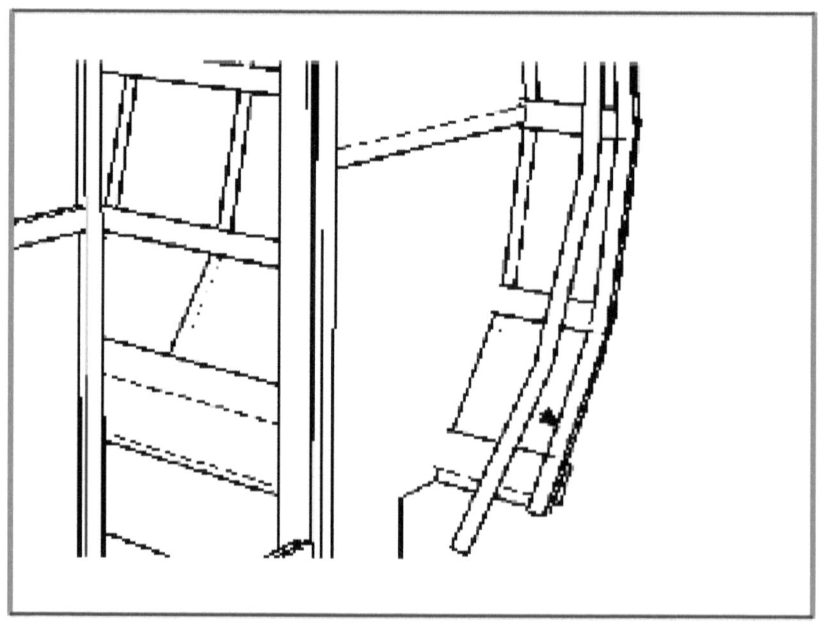

Inner Bow Installation

A second set of ***Inner Bows*** is to be installed immediately next to the first set. The ***Roof Cover*** material will be trapped between the first and second set of bows and will be under the newly installed ***Inner Bow,*** holding it in place. The ***Bow*** is secured with screws that go through the pilot holes in the ***Bow*** and are screwed into the ***Runners***. The cover should be pulled into place so that there is some tension on it as the bow is screwed into place.

Side Weatherboard

Description	Size	Qty
Side Weatherboard	1 x 4 x 9'3"	2

Hardware: 1 1/4" Deck Screws

Tools: Drill, Screw Driver

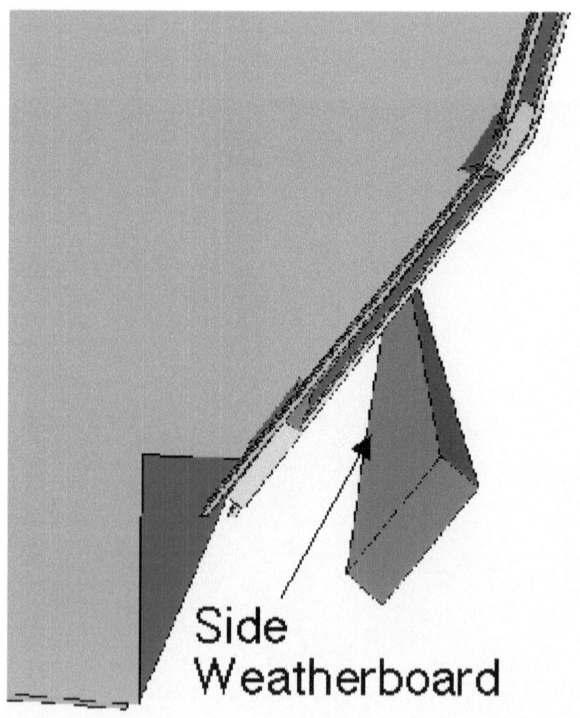

Weatherboard Installation

The 1 x 4 ***Side Weatherboard*** board is aligned with the top of the ***Ledge Runner*** and front edge of the first ***Bow*** and attached using two 6-1 5/8" screws. Screws are used to attach the board to the ***Bows*** and ***Ledge Runner*** at each ***Bow*** location..

When it is attached it should slightly stretch the fabric, and have a smooth appearance.

One advantage of this design is that the cover can be easily replaced by detaching the ***Weatherboards*** and the inner bows and simply installing a new one in an identical way as the old one

Trim Excess Cover Material

Using a sharp utility knife trim the excess ***Roof Cover*** material from the sides and ends using the ***Side Weatherboard*** and ***Inner Bows***, respectively, as guides for cutting.

Door

Description	Size	Qty	Drawing
Door	6 x 2 x 3/8	1	16
Hinges		2	

Tools :Tape Measure, Screw Driver

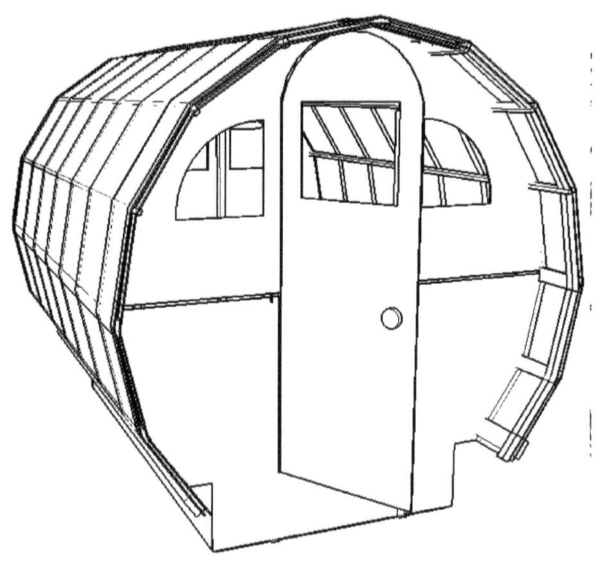

Door Assembly

Since the caravan door is light weight, standard cabinet hinges can be used, as long as they are surface mount hinges. The hinges used in the kit are surface-mount, variable overly, self closing hinges. The self closing hinges tend to keep the door closed without any addition spring or closers, and are easy to install.

Measure along the long side of the ***Door***, about 8 inches from the bottom. Make a mark at the point where the radius at the top of the door stops and where the flat begins. These will be the location points for the hinges.

Turn the ***Door*** with the outer surface facing downward. Place the flange of the hinge so that it is located at the mark and that the edge of the ***Door*** is against the "L" shaped section of the flange. The hinge is attached to the door using the screws supplied with the hinge. Install the second hinge at the second mark, 8 inches from the bottom.

The ***Door*** with its hinges is then attached to the end panel. The ***Door*** is to overlap the door opening by about 3/4 inch, so locate the ***Door*** accordingly.

The hasp, used to lock the door, is installed midway along the door.

Shutter

Parts

Description	Size	Qty	Drawing
Shutter	4 x 1.5 x 3/8	1	17
Hinges		2	

Tools : Tape Measure, Screw Driver

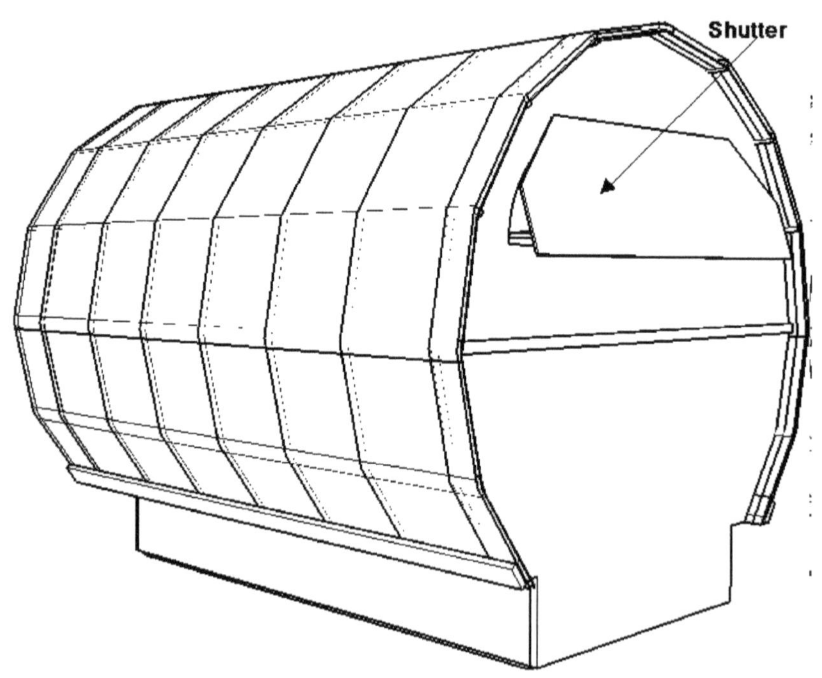

Shutter Assembly

The ***Shutter*** is assembled similarly to the door. The hinges are placed about 8 inches from the ends of the shutter. The larger flange of the hinge is attached to the inner surface of the shutter with the three screws supplied. The **Shutter** is secured to the caravan with the smaller half of the hinge.

Trim

Description	Size	Qty	Drawing
Door Trim	1 x 2 x 6 ft	2	18
Horiz Front Trim	1 x 2 x 2ft	2	
Back Trim	1 x 2 x 6ft.	1	
#6-1″ Wood Screws		12	
1 1/4″ Deck Screws		12	

Tools: Screw Driver,Caulking gun,Chisel

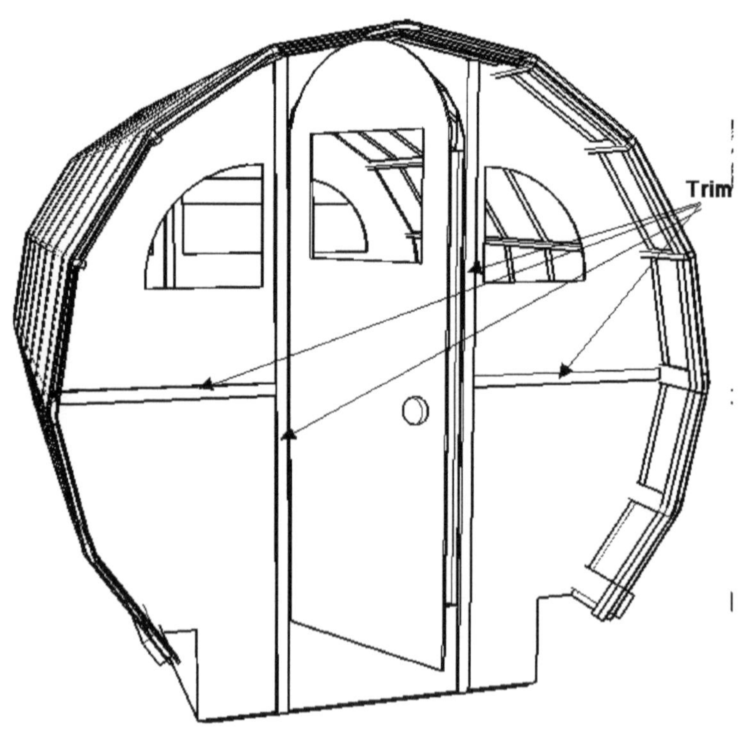

Trim Installation

Ideally the ***Trim*** pieces should be painted before installation. The ***Trim*** is used to cover the seam between the ***Upper*** and ***Lower Rear Panels*** and ***Front Panels*** as well as around the door opening. The ***Vertical Door Trim*** can be attached using #6-1 1/4 inch screws. The trim will interfere somewhat with the door hinges, so it will be necessary to remove some material in this area using a small chisel or knife.

Apply caulking to the horizontal seams on the front and rear before centering the trim pieces and using 1 inch screws to attach them to the Panels.

Hardware

Description	Size	Qty
Door Knob	1 1/2″ dia	1
Hasp		2
Hook and Eye Lock		1 set
Window Screen	15″ x 19″	4

Tools: Screw Driver,

Stapler

Screens for the window openings are necessary for summertime camping, when insects are a nuisance. Screening material, preferably plastic screening is cut to fit the window and simply stapled to the inside of the caravan panels.

The installation of a simple "hook and eye" lock is an effective method of locking the caravan door from the inside. One method of locking it from the outside involves installing a "hasp" on the door and frame. The loop portion of the "hasp" would be mounted on the trim section surrounding the door. The other half of the hasp would be mounted to the door. A small piece of 1/2" wood mounted under neath this portion might be required to compensate for the height differences of the two surfaces. The shutter can be secured with a hasp the same way as the door. A small padlock can be used to secure the interior contents of the caravan when it is unattended, or when it is is "on the road".

Window Shutters

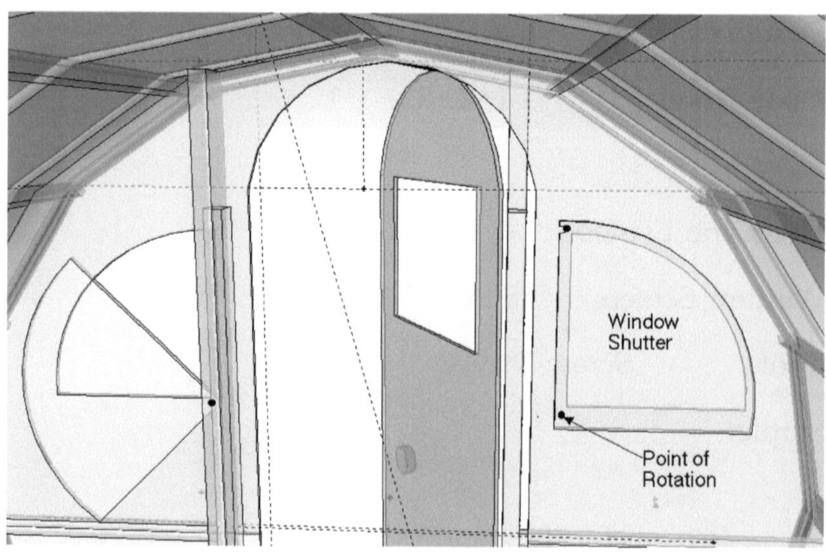

The rear windows and door also require protection against wind and rain. These can be protected using individual shutters that cover the window opening. Although there are a number of possible designs for shut

tering the windows including curtains there is a unique design of shutters for the quarter circle widow on each side of the door opening. These shutters are also quarter circles that are slightly larger than the corresponding windows. They are attached by a 1/4" bolt that goes through the shutter at what would be the approximate center point of the complete circle. The bolt can be secured with a wing nut, which can be loosened and tightened to allow the shutter to be rotated and cover varying portion of the window. At the point of full rotation the edge of the shutter encounters another bolt which fits into a corresponding slot on the shutter. The shutter can be then secured in a closed position for com
plete covering of the window. The shutters can be installed on either the inside or out side of the panel, depending on the situation. It might be better to have it on the outside for storage or for traveling, whereas the inside might be better when the caravan is set up for camping, since it can be adjusted from the inside.

The door window can be shuttered in a unique way as well. In this design, the shutter is hinged at the bottom of the widow opening. To close it, it swings upward and is latched into place. This configuration minimizes problems with the shutter interfering with the outside structure of the caravan, when it is opened or closed. Using spring loaded (self closing) hinges allows the shutter to be easily closed and it remains in the closed position without any latching required. Of course, the door shutter can also be mounted on the outside from the top of the widow, in a more conventional configuration.

The New Gypsy Caravan
Assembly CheckList

Base

__ Attach Connectors(4) to Base Ends(2)
__ Attach Base Ends to Base Sides

Floor*

__ Attach Floor to Base Assembly

Ledges

__ Attach Ledge Runner(2) to Ledge(2)
__ Attach Ledge Assembly to Base Assembly

Base to Trailer*

____ Bolt Base Assembly to Trailer

Lower End Panels

__ Attach Lower End Panels(2) to Base Assembly
__ Attach Glue Block(12) to Panels
__ Attach Ledge Runner to Glue Blocks

King Posts

__ Attach King Posts to Lower Panel with screws

Upper End Panels

__ Attach Upper Panels(2) to King Posts with screws

Runners

__ Attach Glue Blocks to Lower Panel
__ Attach Glue Block to The top of the Upper Panel.
__ Mark Runners for Bow Spacing
__ Mount Lower Runners on Lower Panels
__ Attach Lower Runners with screws to End Blocks
__ Mount Upper Runners to Upper Panels using ad hesive
__ Mount Ridge Runner to Upper Panel
__ Attach Ridge Runner with screws to Glue Block

Bows

__ Attach Bows to Runners using adhesive and screws
__ Caulk End Panels.

Bed *

__ Attach Glue Blocks to Lower Runners
__ Attach Bed Frame Panel to King Posts
__ Attach Bad Frame Panel to Glue Blocks on Run ners
__ Install Bed stretchers into notches on Bed Base

__ Install Bed surface panels

Painting*

__ Sand, Paint and Varnish interior and exterior of the caravan frame

Inner Liner*

__ Fit and Staple inner liner to the bows

Insulation*

__ Fit and staple insulation over the inner liner and to the bows

Roof Cover

__ Fit and staple to cover to the bows on both ends and underneath the ledge.

Inner Bows

__ Secure the cover on both ends using by attaching I nner Bows to the bows on the ends

Weatherboard

__ Secure the cover to the Ledge by attaching the Weatherboard with screws along the bottom edge of the Ledge.

__ Trim excess material from cover

Door

__ Install door in door opening using hinges.

__ Install a hasp on the exterior and a hook and eye lock in the interior

__ Install a door knob to the exterior

Shutter

__ Install the large shutter over the rear window openings using hinges

__ Install a hasp to allow the shutter to be locked

__ Attach chain or thin rope to shutter and attach a screw eye to the outer bow.

Trim and Finish

__ Using screws, attach trim to the exterior panels over the seams and along the door frame

__ Staple Screening over windows

Window shutters*

__ Using nuts and bolts attach triangular shutters to the interior of the windows

- *Optional*

•

Getting the Caravan on the Trailer

If the caravan was not built on the trailer, it will need to be placed there. The completed caravan will weigh around 250-300 pounds. Although this is not heavy for a camping trailer like this, it still is a job to get it on a trailer. You will require at least one, and preferably two other people to help. The method I used employed an inexpensive 2 ton "come-along". To use it, we wrapped a rope around the base of the caravan several times and tied the rope in a knot leaving some slack. The next thing we did was to position the caravan next to the open end of the trailer. We then tilted the trailer so that the tongue was in the air. We lifted the end of the caravan onto the back edge of the trailer . If you had enough help, it might be possible to push the caravan up the tilted trailer. We attached the "come-along" by its hook to the ropes surrounding the base and the cable end to the trailer tongue. We were able to winch the caravan almost half way along the length of the trailer. At that point it was relatively easy to push it the rest of the way until it was positioned at the end of the trailer body. If the winch is still required, it can be repositioned and used again to complete the job.

Before You Go.

Make sure the wheels and tires are in good condition and that the tires are properly inflated. Tire problems can occur when the trailer is used only occasionally and tires degrade in the sunlight or slowly lose pressure.

A tongue jack is a great accessory to have. These are adjustable and allow to trailer to be leveled when it is not installed on the vehicle.

Some sort of support is required for the rear end of the trailer, so that the trailer does not rise up every time someone goes through the door. The first time it happens it is a very disconcerting experience. After that , it is just annoying. I have propped up my caravan with pieces of firewood or concrete block brought along for the purpose. Now, I use an old automobile scissors jack for the purpose. It has the advantage of being adjustable as well.

Make sure the wheel bearings are properly lubricated.

Always carry a spare tire. Tires on lower cost utility trailer are prone to failure, and being caught with a flat tire on a freeway 2000 miles from home, with all of your belonging in your caravan is not a fun ,way to spend a vacation.

Safety and Hook-Up Procedures

Prior to hook-up, check hitch on tow vehicle.

Check for loose bolts, attaching pins, etc.

Check ball for proper torque and size to match trailer coupler.

When receiver hitch is used, check cross pin and safety pin.

Check electrical connector plug on vehicle.

Visually check for loose or frayed wires hanging from plug and where connected to tow vehicle wiring.

Using test light or test stand, check for electric current in plug at the proper pin location in the plug.(Marker lights, Left turn, Right turn, Brake, Ground and Auxiliary hot wire, if applicable)

Hook trailer to tow vehicle.

Check for proper ball size to match trailer hitch coupler, verify coupler securely attached to ball and insert safety pin.

Attach safety chains to tow vehicle.(Chains must be hooked to a permanent member of the tow vehicle. The addition of eyes or loops may be necessary to accommodate the safety chain properly.)

Check trailer for proper towing altitude. A loaded or unloaded trailer must be towed with a positive hitch height for a safe towing.

When the hook-up is slightly higher compared to the leveling of the trailer, a smoother performance is given.

Connect electrical plug, check lights by verifying on trailer as follows.

Check marker light (running lights) with only park lights on. If interior dome lights are applicable, they should be tested now to see if they are wired in conjunction with marker lights on the trailer.

Turn off tow vehicle park lights, then turn on left turn signal and verify on the trailer.

Turn off left turn signal, then turn on right turn signal and verify on the trailer.

With turn signals and park lights at the off position, apply pressure to the brake pedal on the towing vehicle and verify that the brake (stop) lights are working.

Check all tires for proper inflation.

Check tire side wall for recommended pressure.

Check all lug nuts for proper torque.

During the life of the trailer, it is recommended to periodically check lug nut torque.

Check all doors and latches. Door should be closed and latched during towing.

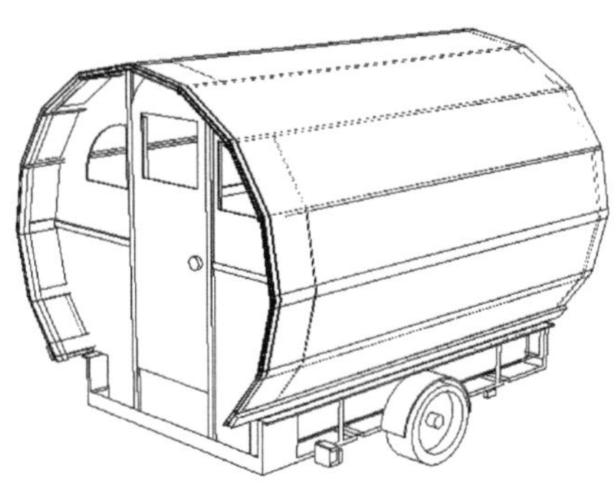

Sources

Trailers and Equipment

Harbor Freight
www.harborfreight.com

Tractor Supply
www.mytcstore.com

Trailer Plans

www.synhx.com

Insulation

Reflectix

www. reflectixinc.com/

Home Depot

www.homedepot.com

Roof Covering

Lowes

www.lowes.com

Camping Supplies (Dutch Ovens, Tripods)

Campmor

www.campmor.com

Hardware

Amerock

www.amerock.com

Bibliography

Fonseca,Isabel, ***Bury Me Standing.*** New York, Vintage Books, 1999

Lloyd, Walter, ***How to Build a Bow Top,*** Kendad, Cumbria, Woodsmanship Ltd.,1999

Pearson, David, ***Freewheeling Homes,*** White River Junction, Vermont,Chelsea Green Publishing Company,2002

Pearson, David, ***Circle Homes,*** WhiteRiver Junction, Vermont,Chelsea Green Publishing Company,2001

Thompson, John, ***Making Model Gypsy Caravans,*** Knights Hill Square, London, W. Hobby Limited, 1997

Ward-Jackson, H. And Harvey, Denis E., ***The English Gypsy Caravan,*** Great Britain,Country Book Club, 1973

Wilson, Carol, ***Gypsy Feast,*** Hippocrene Books, Inc., New York,2004

American Gypsy Caravan

Specification

Length	9′ 3″
Width	6′0″″
Height	6″2″
Floor	8′ x 4′
Bed Area	6′0″ x 4′0″
Weight	275#

<u>Construction</u>

Base	1″x12″ Pine
Runners	1″x 2″ Pine
Bows	1/4″ x 1 1/2″ poplar
End Panels	3/8″ plywood
Floor	3/4″ plywood
Roof Covering	10 mil reinforced PE
Windows	5 screened with adjustable shutters

THE NEW GYPSY CARAVAN
Materials List

Material (purchased)	Qty	Cut Lngth	Comments
2"x3" x 6'	4	6'	King Posts
1" x 12" x 8'	5	8'	Base sides ,Ledges
1" x12"x 2'	2	3" 10 1/2	Base ends
1" x 4" x 10'	1	9' 3"	Ridge runner,Weatherboards
1" x 3" x 10'	8	9' 3"	Lower runner
1" x 2" x 10'	6	9' 3"	Roof runners
1"x 2" x 8'	2	6'	Vertical Trim
	2'	2'	Horizontal Trim
1" x 2" x6'	1	6'	Horizontal Trim(rear)
*1/4" x 2" x 8"	20	87"	Outer Bows
	8	87"	Inner Bows
*3/8 BC plywood	5	custom	End panels Door,shutters
¾ CDPlywood			Floor1
Bed Kit (optional)			
**3/8"BC plywood	2shts	custom	Bed frames
2"x2"x 8'	4	48"	Bed supports

-

Misc

Glue Blocks(basic)	1 x 3 x 3 1/2"	(8)
Glue Blocks (bed)	1 x 3 x 3 1/2" (6)	
Base Connectors	2" x 2" x 11 1/2"	(4)

Roof Covering
10' x 16' — 10 mil reinforced PE, or woven polyester canvas
Insulation(optional) — 10' x 16' or equivalen
Roof Liner — 10' x 16' -Plaid

-

Hardware
Galvanized Deck Screws
1" #6
1 1/4"
1 5/8"

Hinges		4	Door and shutters
Hook and eye set	1 set		Interior Door lock
Hasps		2	Exterior Door and shutter lock

* Included in Basic Caravan Kit

** Included in Bed kit

Drawings

Drawing 01 Base Components

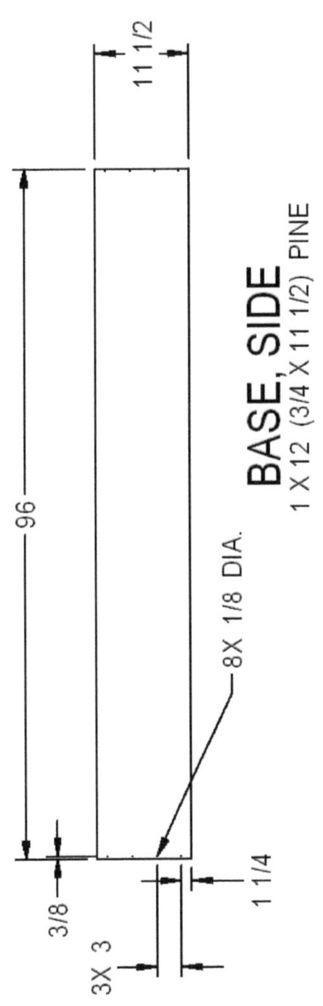

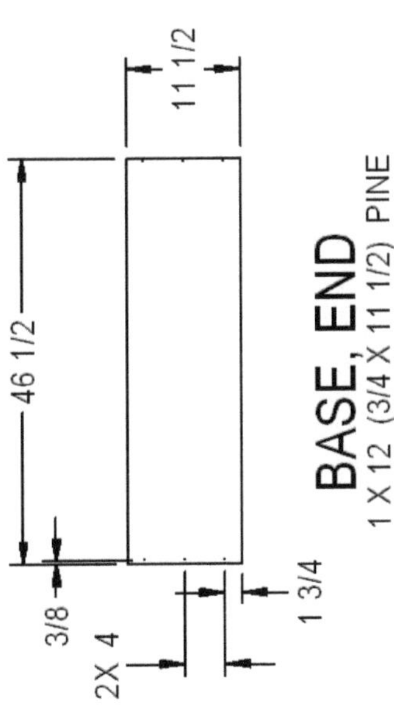

Drawing 02 Glue and Connector Blocks

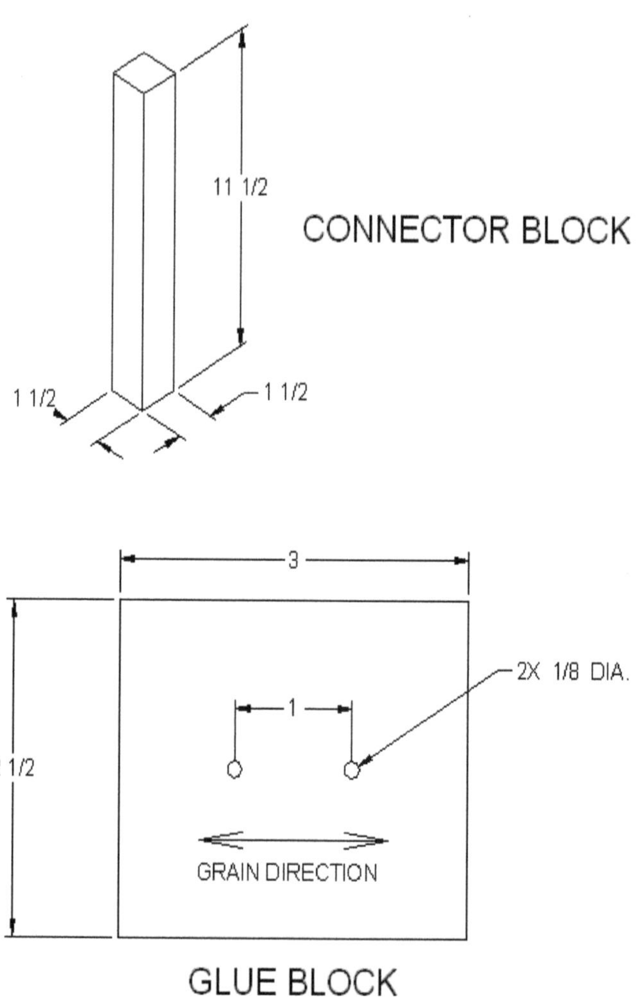

Drawing 03 -Floor

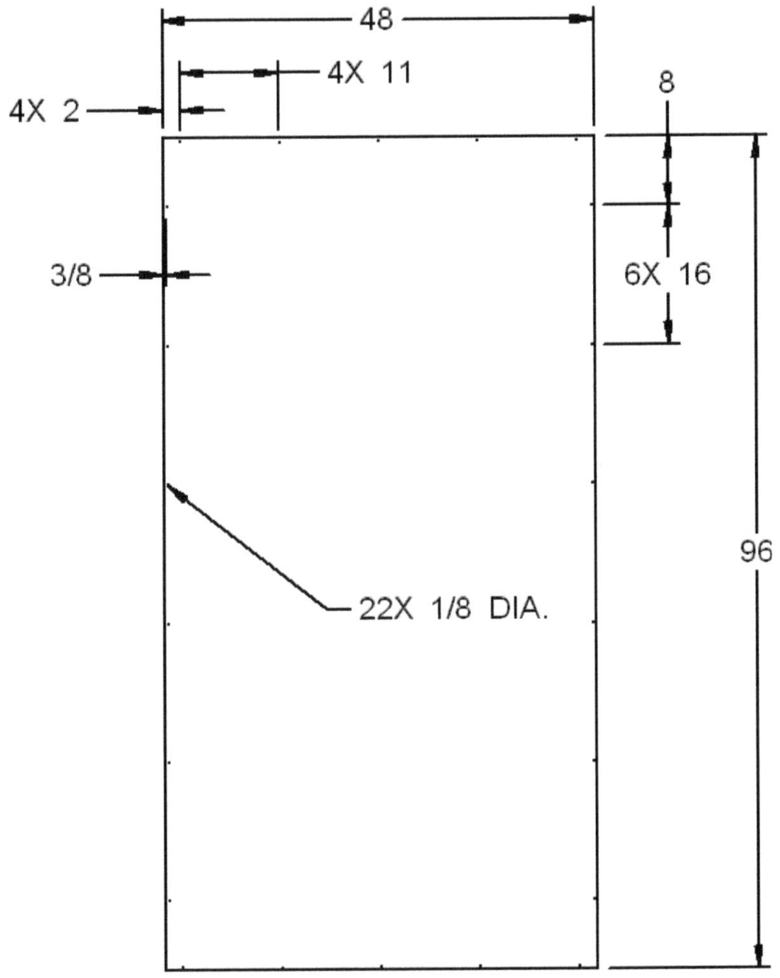

PLYWOOD FLOOR

MAT'L: 3/4" EXTERIOR GRADE PLYWOOD

Drawing 04 Ledge

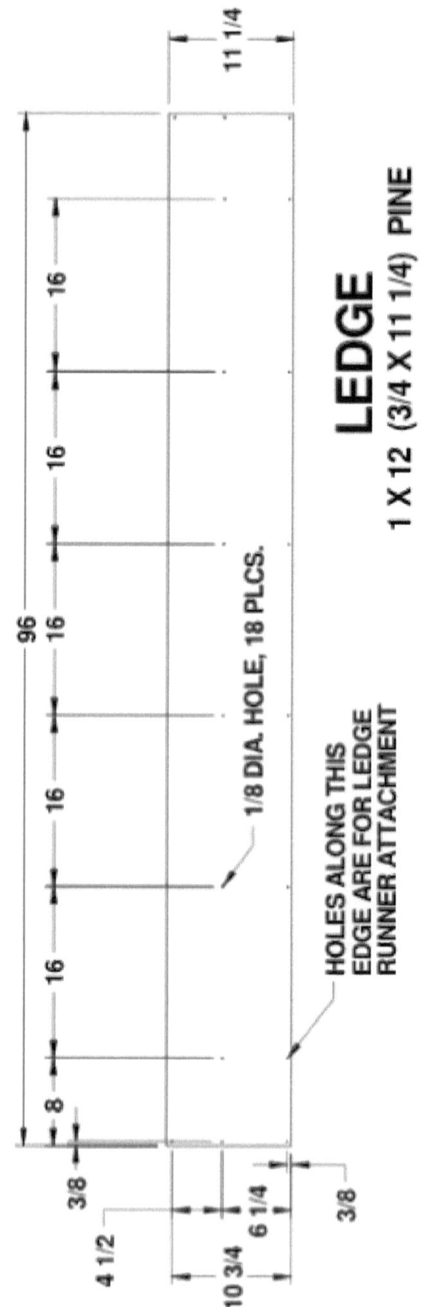

Drawing 05 King Post

Drawing 06 Lower Rear Panel

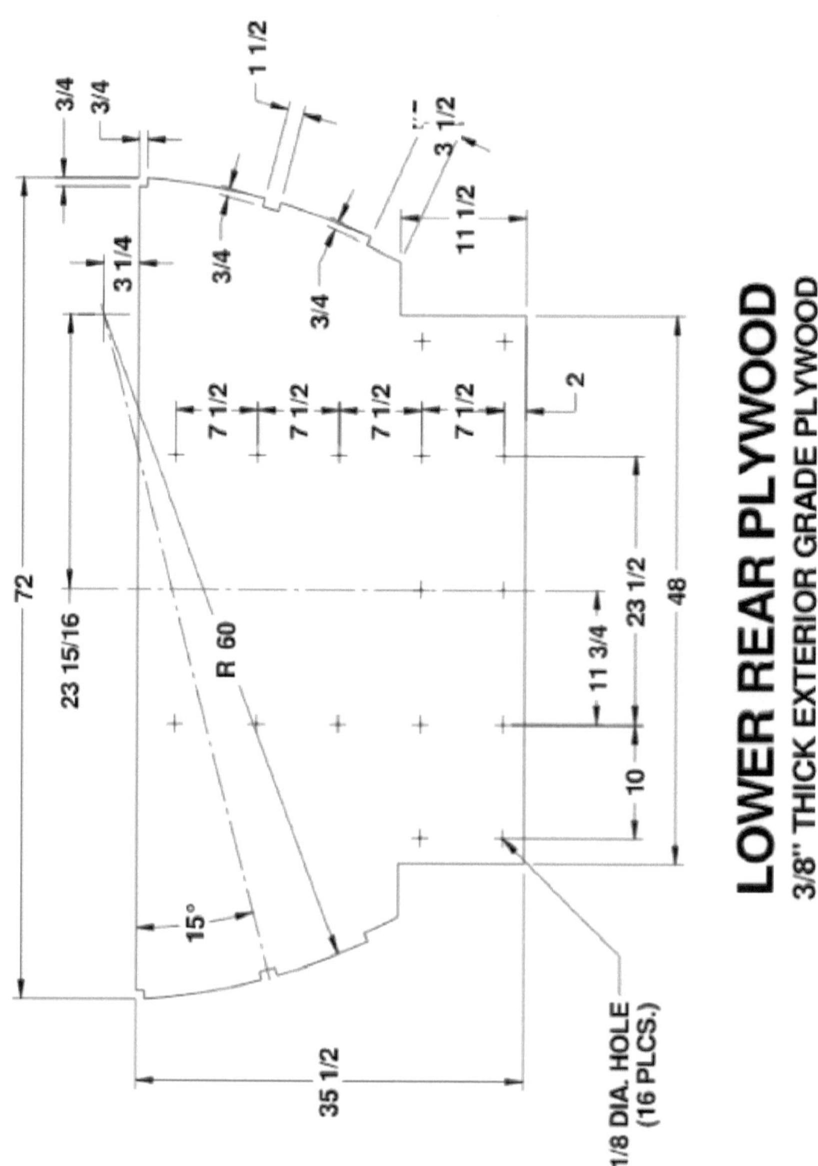

Drawing 07 - Lower Front Panel

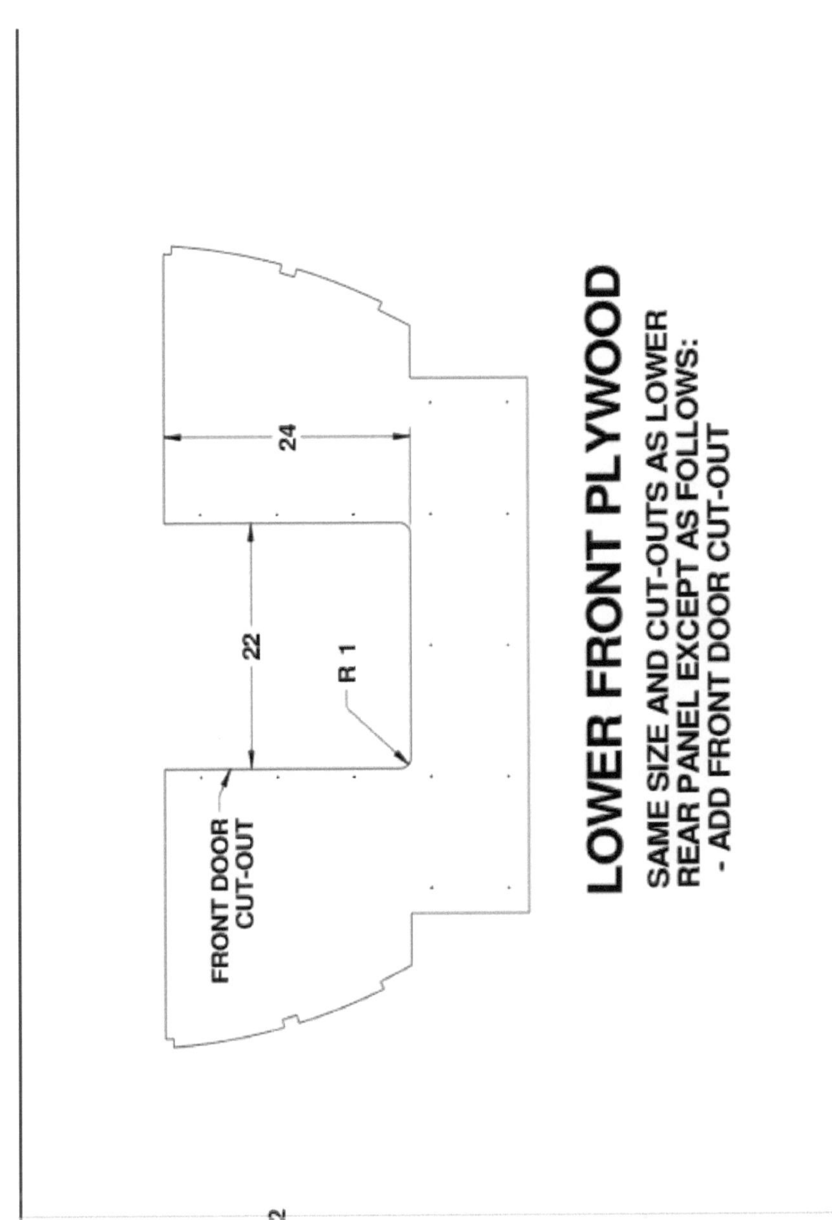

Drawing 08 Upper Rear Panel

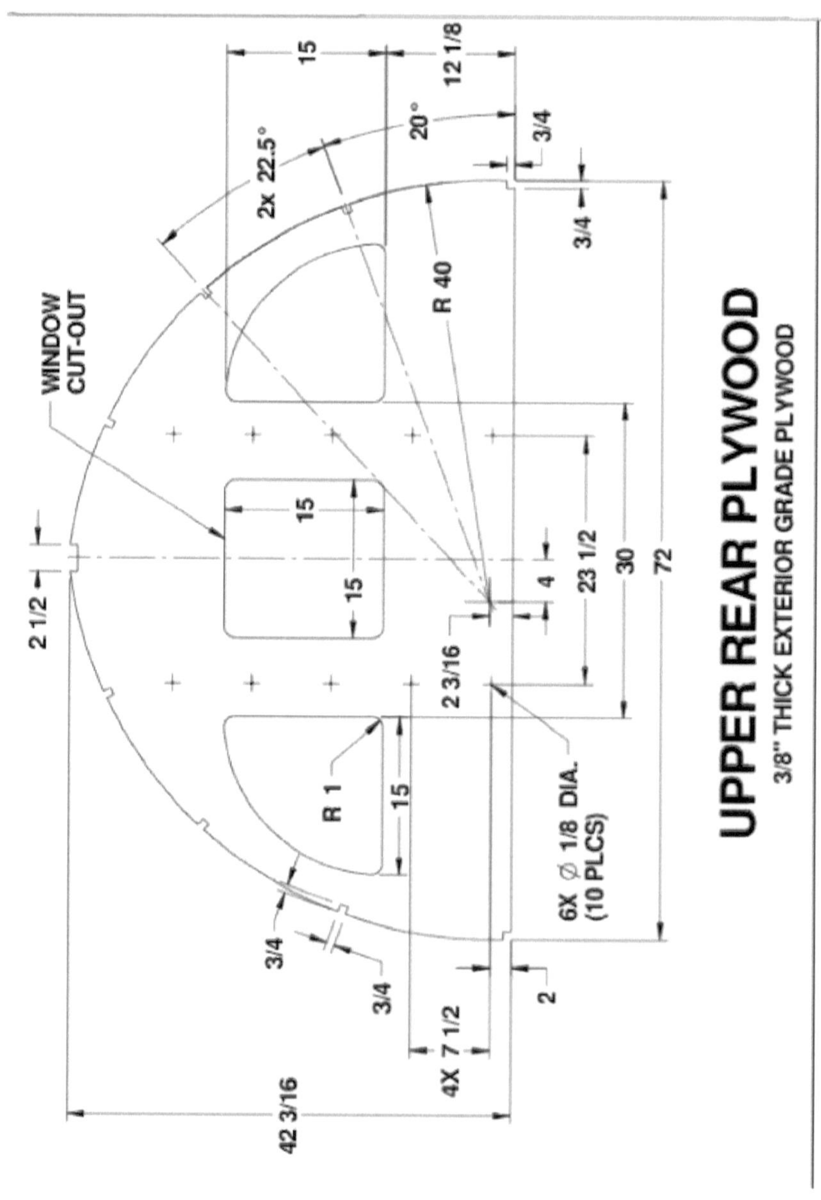

Drawing 09 Upper Front Panel

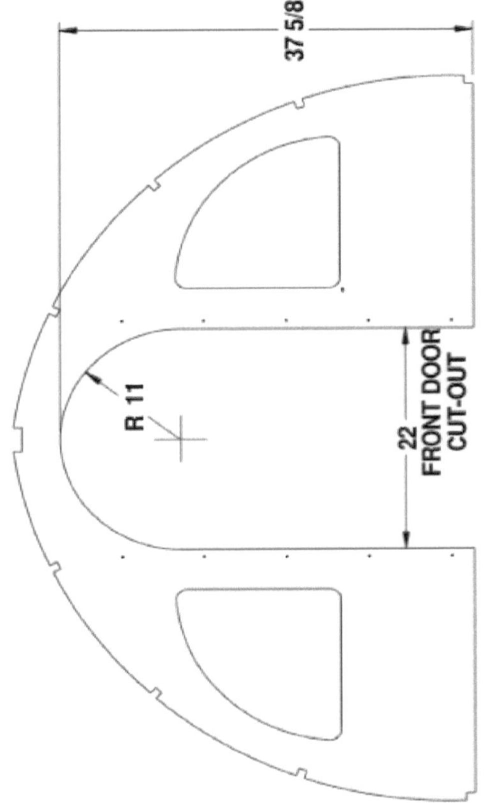

Drawing 10 Ridge Runner and Lower Roof Runners

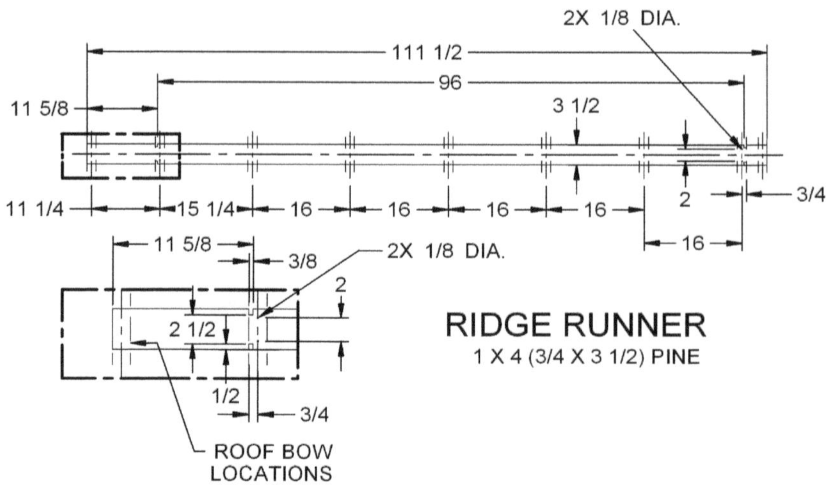

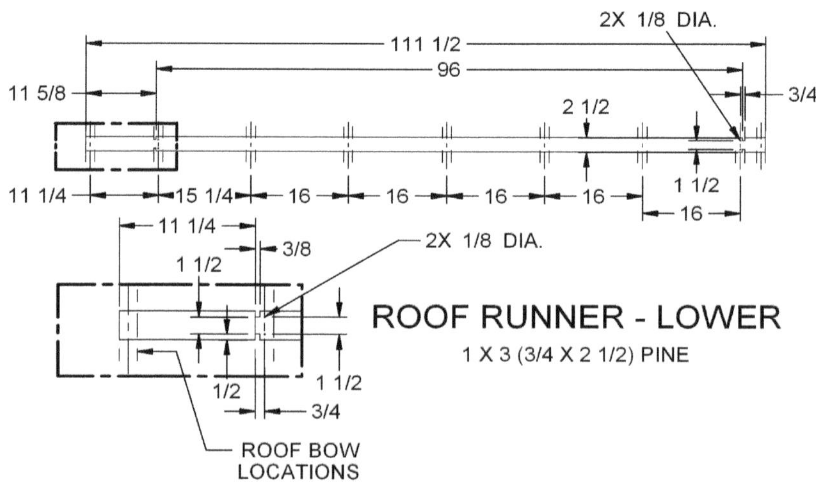

Drawing 11 Upper Roof and Ledge Runners

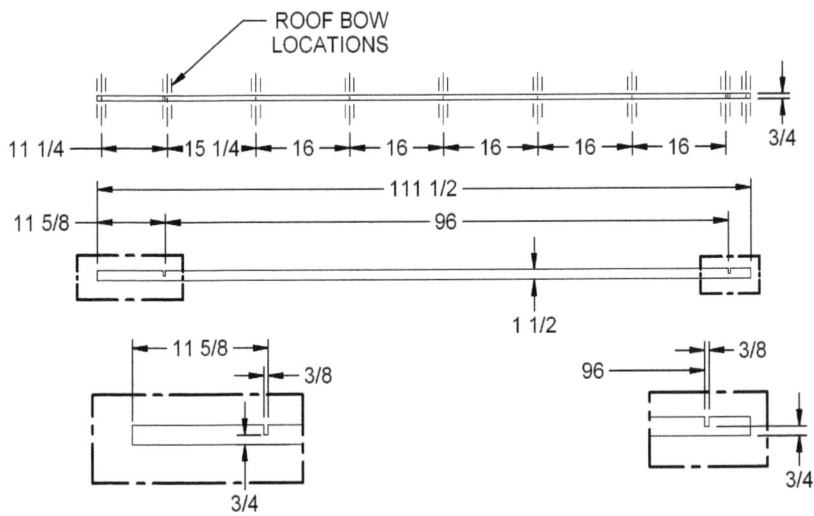

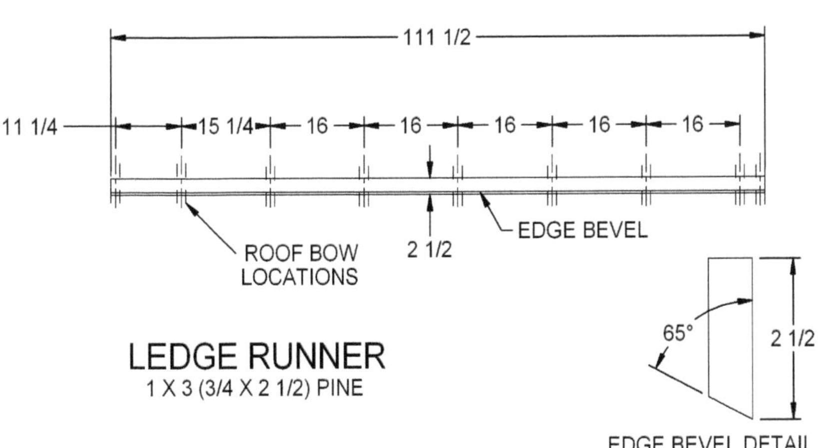

Drawing 12 Outer Bow

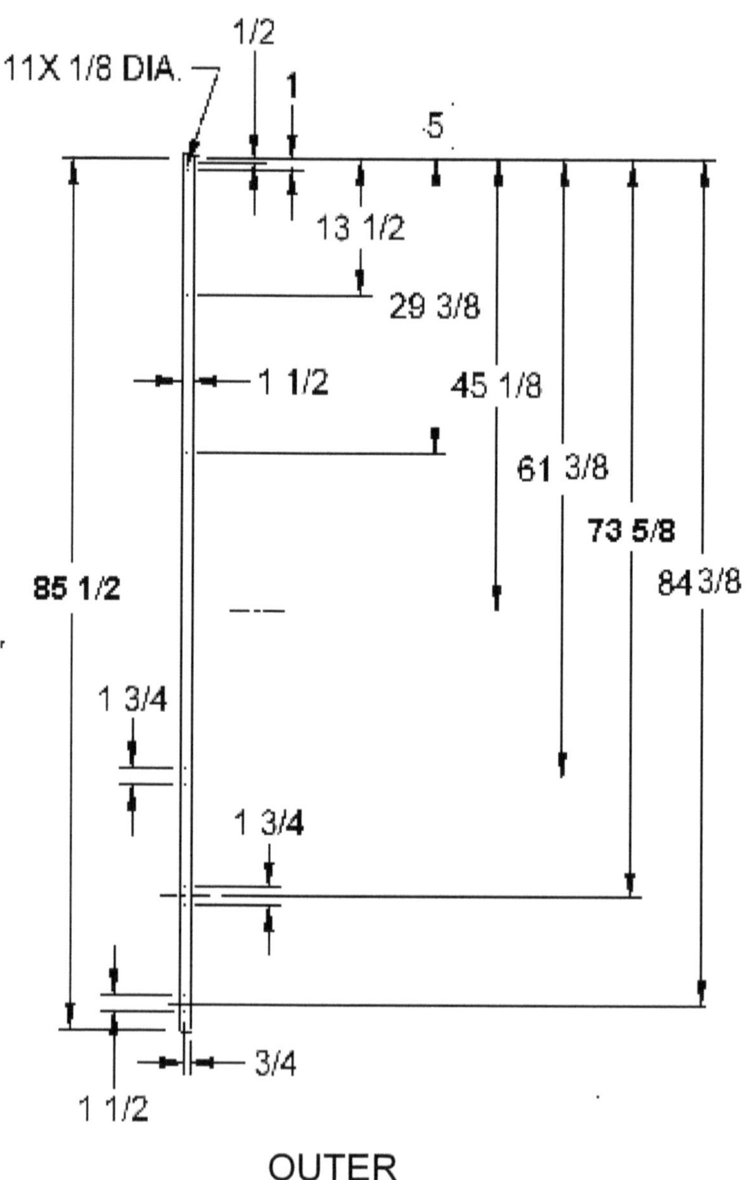

Drawing 13 Inner Bow

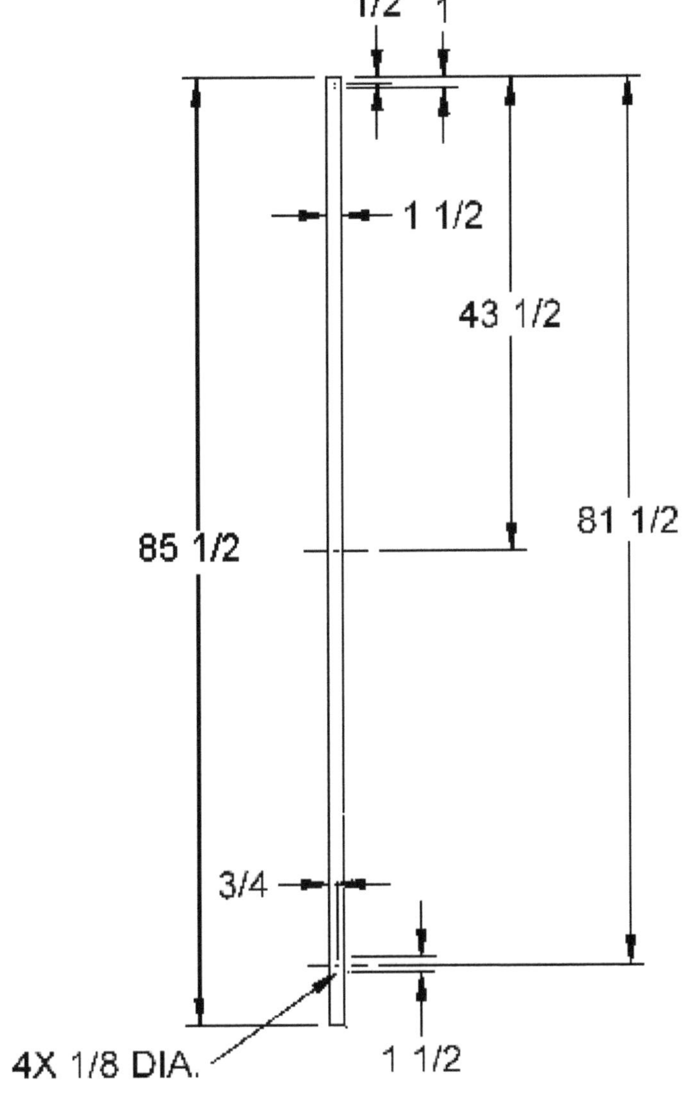

INNER
ROOF BOW

Drawing 14 Weatherboard

Drawing 15 Door

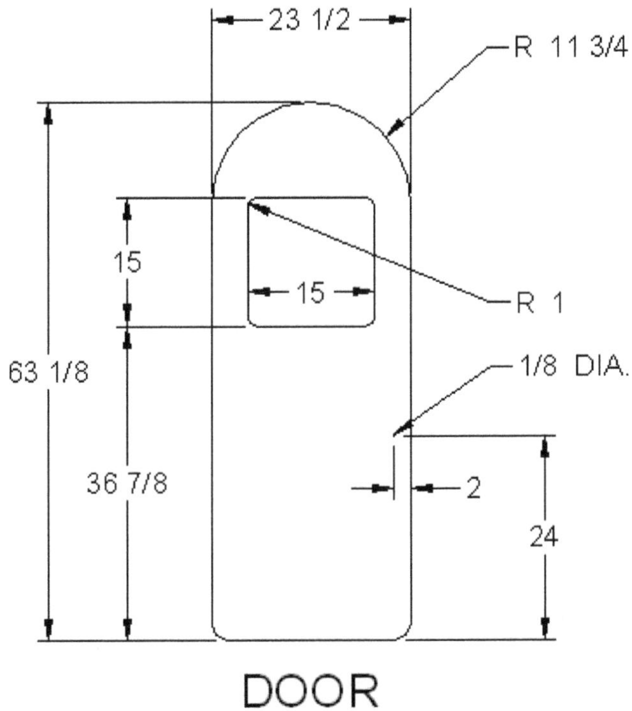

Drawing 16 Shutters

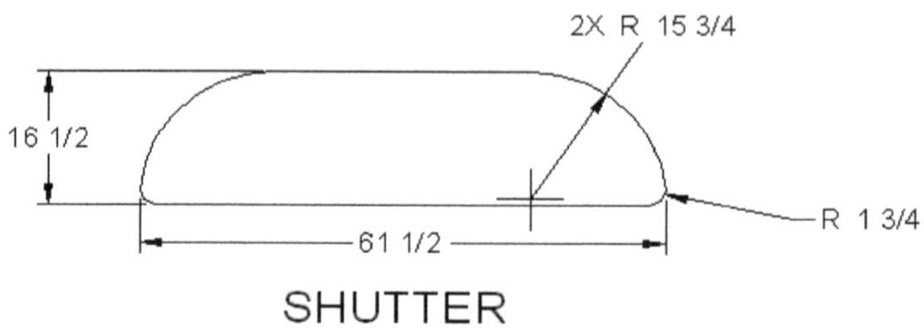

Drawing 17 Trim

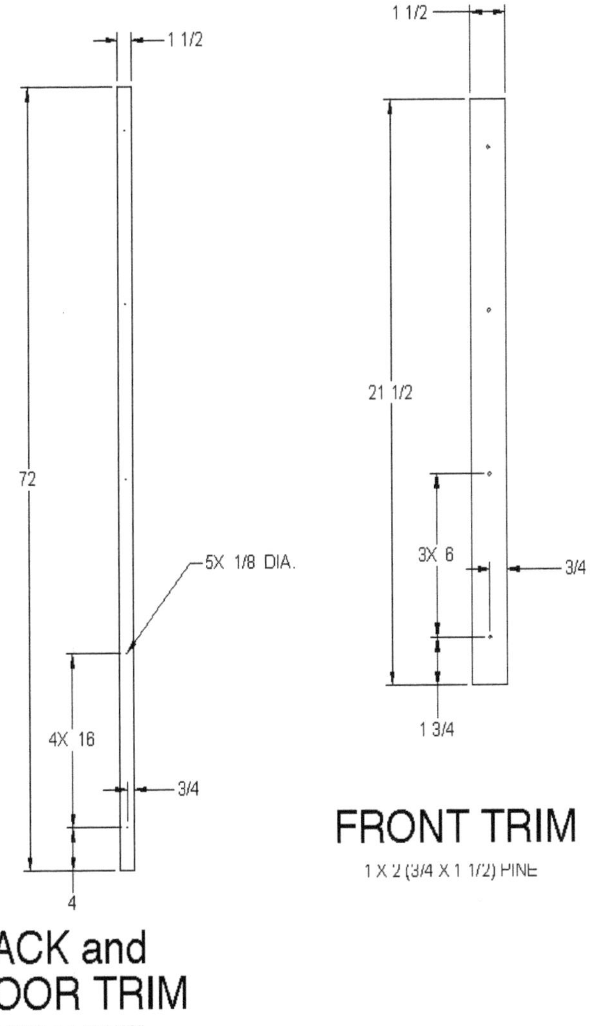

Drawing 18 Bed Support Panel

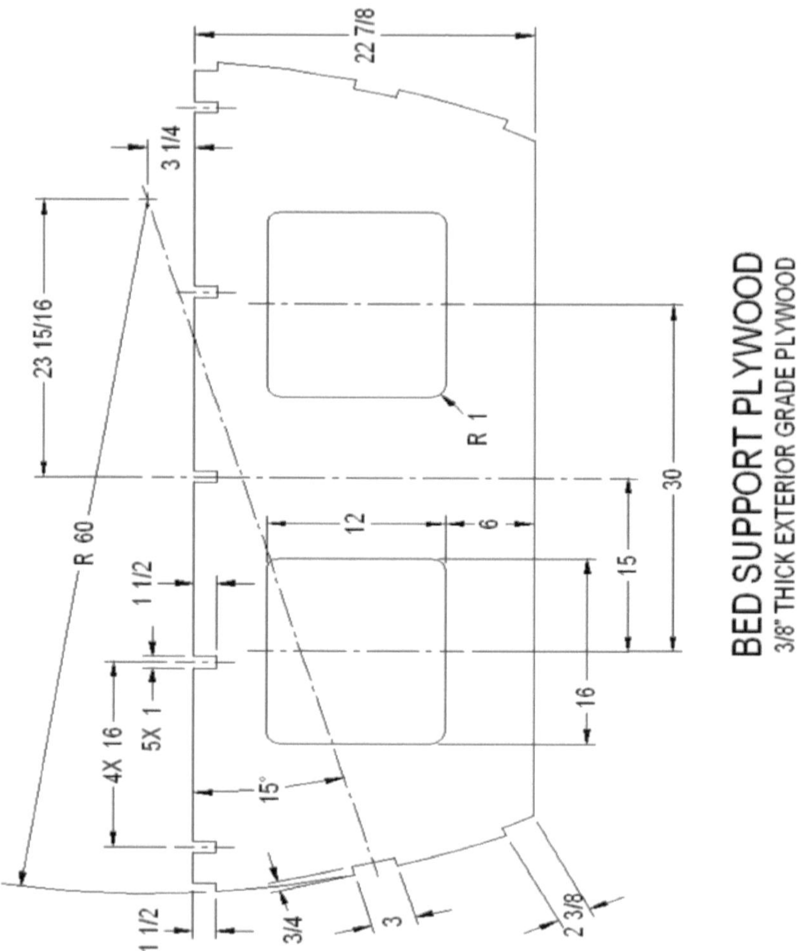

Drawing 19 Bed Stretchers

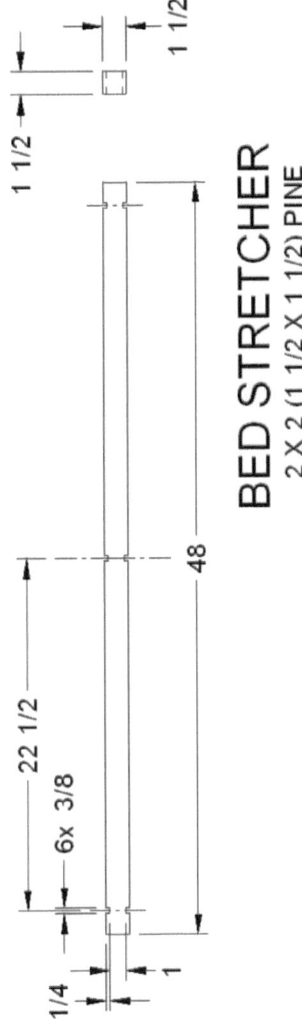

AMERICAN VARDO

Information on Gypsy Art, Music and Literature is available on http://www.amvardo.com/things

Kits, plans and books are available on http://www.amvardo.com/caravan .

Updates and further information on "The New Gypsy Caravan" will be available on the website.

Kosko bokht

www.ingramcontent.com/pod-product-compliance
Ingram Content Group UK Ltd.
Pitfield, Milton Keynes, MK11 3LW, UK
UKHW040559210726
13854UKWH00008B/1545